Hope
for Judas

Hope
for Judas

God's Boundless Mercy for Us All

Christoph Wrembek, S.J.

New City Press
Hyde Park, New York

Published in the United States by New City Press
202 Comforter Blvd., Hyde Park, NY 12538
www.newcitypress.com
© 2021 New City Press (English translation)

Translated by Marianne Hessing
from the original German edition *Judas, der Freund*
© 2019 Neue Stadt Verlag, Munich, Germany

Cover photo by Jean-Claude Gadreau, Vézelay © 2021
Cover design and layout by Miguel Tejerina

Library of Congress Control Number: 2020952426

ISBN: 978-1-56548-381-1
ISBN: 978-1-56548-383-5 e-book

Printed in the United States of America

Contents

A word to the readers

The little book offers more than you might assume at first glance. Maybe you found the title to be somewhat surprising: "Hope for Judas" . . .

Judas? The son of destruction?

Judas, about whom the Gospels tell us very little beyond the dramatic events in the course of the Passion, in him, Jesus' loving-saving action finds its culmination?

Drawing from a depiction on the beautifully carved top of a column (in architectural terms, a capital[1]) in the medieval Basilica of St. Mary Magdalene in the town of Vézelay, France, much is awaiting you: a breathtaking, enlightening and, no doubt, oftentimes touching journey through different core stories of sacred scripture. Stories about being lost, but ultimately always stories about salvation. Be patient and let yourself be taken on a tour into the soul of the Gospel, which is Jesus himself. A treasure chest of faith, of spirituality and of direction might open for your life.

What does the book offer you? You will come to know the fascinating story of the origin of this capital, you will

---

1. A "capital" is the upper part, or the head, of a pillar or column. The term derives from Latin *capitellum*, literally "little head." For images of the capital in Vézelay, turn to the picture on page 127, and the close-up picture on the bottom of page 15.

accompany Jesus in his encounter with the woman at Jacob's well, and you will discover in a new way the parables of the three "lost ones" – the lost son, the lost sheep and the lost coin. You will find out that there is much to be discovered in Jesus' interactions with Zacchaeus, with the tax collector, and with the crippled woman.

All these encounters and stories can be read in view of Judas. In all of them, the motif of salvation shines through, salvation for even the most *lost* soul of all, because the Creator does not give up on anyone.

Salvation and redemption, therefore, also for Judas? At the end of this booklet you will find a surprising answer. Wonderful and heartening. Carved in stone in the unique depiction of the "Good Shepherd of Vézelay." Visible to the eye, palpable to the heart.

Therein lies an incredible hope. Whichever way our own life may have taken, with all its inconsistencies, we, too, may be able to say in the end: "You, who have taken Judas home, carry me, too!" And if we are not able to bring ourselves to say these words – HE carries home also the one who cannot speak. Everyone. Me, too.

Introduction

For years, I have been captivated by a picture. It occupies a prominent place in my study. It accompanies my thinking and my musing, my theological reflecting, and my personal prayer. It nourishes my loving and, like a deep well, is ever new. The picture shows a capital, the artistically carved top of a column. It is found in the Romanesque abbey church of St. Mary Magdalene in the town of Vézelay, in Burgundy, France. On the left side of the artistic depiction we see Judas who has hanged himself, and to the right, a shepherd who carries the dead Judas over his shoulder, like the lost sheep. I call it "the Good Shepherd of Vézelay." It became the inspiration for this book.

Almost 900 years old, this medieval capital deserves more than just a quick glance. It deserves all our attention because it contains the whole of God's message of salvation and redemption. We are seeing the very being and the very heart of Christian theology, in a way words could not convey any more beautifully, any more powerfully, or any more touchingly.

Just think: In earlier centuries, people had neither binoculars nor cameras. Surely only very few would even have looked up that far to the top of a column, in the shadow of the ceiling. There were many other images to look at, bathed in more light than this one. The unknown sculptor of this capital, his senses imbued with a faith yearning for truth, had created something that remained unnoticed, hidden in the protective shadow. It was too high and too distant.

In our days this seemingly plain yet profoundly expressive image of our faith gets much more attention. It adorns booklets or serves as an image for meditation for those who are searching. Important experts did discover it but did not "notice" its significance. In many art guides, it is not even mentioned since there seems to be nothing important in it. Other capitals in the Basilica of St. Mary Magdalene seem more interesting, even though their themes and symbolic meaning are often not easily understood. Instead, the message of this depiction is immediately evident. The Good Shepherd, Jesus, as he identified himself, is carrying Judas home like the lost sheep. Most scenes on the church's capitals capture themes from the Old Testament or from mythology, but this well-known motif of Jesus, the Good Shepherd, undoubtedly belongs to the New Testament.

This unfamiliar and unusual depiction can be contrasted with another image of Judas. This other image is found only fifty-six miles southeast of Vézelay in the church of St. Lazarus in Autun, built around the same time as the Basilica of St. Mary Magdalene, between 1120 and 1140 CE. The patrons of the two churches, Mary Magdalene and Lazarus, were siblings but the two depictions of Judas in them have nothing in common! In the school of Gislebert, the sculptor who so richly decorated St. Lazarus, Judas is depicted as hanged and at his feet, on his right and left, two satanic demons hungrily crave their prey. In the Vézelay basilica, the unknown sculptor shows the opposite. He does not depict Satan and his demons taking the hanged Judas as prey with them to hell, but rather the Good Shepherd who carries Judas home like a trophy.

In Vézelay, an overall plan for the images in St. Mary Magdalene has never been found, but the preparatory work for the capitals is assumed to have been done by a significant scholar of the time. Research points to Peter the Venerable, an impressive personality of his century. At age twenty-one (in 1115) he was named Prior of the Cloister in Vézelay, and at twenty-eight he became the ninth abbot of the Abbey Cloister of Cluny, the center of the medieval renewal movement of monastic life. He had great human sensitivity, was deeply pious and theologically outstanding (he had the Qur'an translated into Latin), and he gave asylum in Cluny to another brilliant loner of his time: Peter Abelard.

If Peter the Venerable indeed gave inspiration to the capitals, we need to ask if Peter Abelard's life-journey could have been a vivid inspiration for this unique depiction of Judas. So, allow me to take you on an expedition, a brief summary of this fascinating story.

Abelard prided himself in being a great philosopher and master in dialectics, the debating of the truth of opinions. In 1115, he taught in Paris. The great crowds of students who followed him confirmed him in his vain self-image. This necessarily led to opposition, even more so since Abelard attempted to integrate reason with faith. Among his students was Héloïse, extremely gifted intellectually as well as extraordinarily beautiful, the niece of the influential Canon Fulbert. She, too, admired and adored the philosopher. After an initial serious, morally correct teacher-student relationship, Abelard discovered that aside from dialectics and logic, sensual pleasures had also awakened in him. Thus, Héloïse and Abelard became one of the most famous, most scandalous, and most incomprehensible pair of lovers in history. Both were aflame for each other with body, spirit, and soul. Héloïse loved him from the beginning with a passionate (and as time would show), lifelong and unconditional love. They soon became a couple.

When she bore him a son, Abelard sent her away to his family. His sensuality had not grown into responsible love even though, to appease Fulbert, he married Héloïse sacramentally. In punishment for what Abelard had done to his family's reputation, Héloïse's outraged father clandestinely sent men to have him castrated.

At Abelard's insistence, for her protection but against her own wishes, Héloïse entered the convent. Even though far removed and without contact for many years, her love for the beloved never diminished. Eventually, she became the Abbess of the Paraclete Cloister, founded by Abelard.

Humiliated though he was, Abelard continued teaching. In 1141, not without intrigue, and with the consent of Bernard of Clairvaux, the Synod of Sens declared Abelard a heretic. He was now a broken man, all vanity extinguished. He became known as a great sinner, a heretic excluded from the Church. His life was destroyed and hopeless. He initially planned to go to Rome to appeal to the pope. However, he set out for Cluny where Peter the Venerable was Abbot. His pilgrimage to Cluny led him through the town of Vézelay, where a year before the church had been completed, still without the narthex (the entrance hall). We may wonder . . . did he enter there and look up to his right? Did he recognize himself in Judas, the one who in his hopelessness had hanged himself? Did he see the shepherd too . . .? Yet unlike Judas, Abelard had not handed Jesus over; he even sought, like his master, to bring reason into faith. He did not hang himself, but public opinion of the day had "hanged" him, so to speak.

He knocked at the door in Cluny and together with beggars and pilgrims asked for a bed. But Peter the Venerable recognized who was seeking refuge with him and welcomed him in honor. Just one year later, on April 21, 1142, Abelard died. Peter the Venerable had the greatness and freedom of soul to personally inform Abelard's rightful wife, by now Abbess Heloise ("my dearest sister in our Lord") of the passing of "the man who belongs to you." At the end of his letter to the Abbess, he wrote: "He, to whom you are joined through the bond of the flesh, then through the firmer and stronger bond of divine love, he, with whom and under whom you consecrated yourself to the service of God, he, I say, will today be embraced instead of by you, by God in love, as your other self. And on the day of the coming of the Lord, at the voice of the archangel, at the sound of the trumpet which announces the highest judge coming down from heaven, he in his grace will return him to you – he will keep him for you."

Héloïse requested Abelard's body from the Abbey in Cluny, and Peter the Venerable had the corpse *discreetly* taken from the cemetery, accompanying it himself to the wife, the Abbess of the Paraclete Cloister. Once more he had to pass through Vézelay, maybe looking up to the capital he had probably given inspiration to, seeing the Good Shepherd carrying home on his shoulders the greatest of all sinners. Thus, he now carried Abelard home – until God would give him back to his wife.

Just think: the Good Shepherd carries not *any* man, but Judas, "the son of destruction!" The one, who, according to tradition, could not be redeemed. Yet it is not tradition that has the last word, but God.

In this book, I want to look at the question: how did Jesus treat sinners? Did he exclude them because of their sins and say: "You do not deserve that I have communion with you and you with me. You need to first do penance and repent!"? Didn't Jesus also threaten? Didn't he say something about being "thrown into the everlasting fire of hell, where Satan and his angels are awaiting?"

Surely being Christian means leading a life in conformity with the call we have received, day after day, from morning to night. Only then can one refer, just as the Church herself does, to Jesus Christ and his Gospel. And what happens with those who, while confessing in words to be Christian, act and lead a life to the contrary in fundamental things, in ways that are clearly against what Jesus intended? Do not those who refuse to forgive another act against Jesus' teaching? Do not ones who act like this, in these cases, have no more communion with Jesus, the Messiah?

What about Judas, the prototype of all sinners?

Hovering above this book, high above and at the same time directly in front of our eyes, is the image of the "Good Shepherd of Vézelay." He carries home Judas, the greatest of all sinners. But there is something special that the unknown sculptor added to his picture, a unique treasure which, it seems to me, has not been discovered by anyone up to now. And it is improbable that Peter the Venerable would have been able to transmit something of such subtlety to the sculptor, had he been the one who gave inspiration to this capital. I believe it must have come from the artist himself. In earlier centuries though, no one could have discovered this subtlety.

When I discovered it, I froze.

At the end of this book I will make visible, truly visible to the eye, what the profound, surely mystically gifted sculptor depicted so beyond the obvious, nearly 900 years ago. It is a most beautiful expression of theology, carved in stone. It is the whole Gospel – perhaps bigger and better than words could ever express.

Hannover, on the Feast of
St. Mary Magdalene, Apostle, 2017

Christoph Wrembek, S.J.

Top right: depiction of Judas in St. Lazarus/Autun
Bottom right: depiction of Judas in St. Mary Magdalene/Vézelay

Jesus and the woman who was divorced five times

In Jesus' parable of the rich man and Lazarus, Abraham (it is God's voice speaking through him) calls the rich, self-absorbed man "my child," like a compassionate caring father who suffers with him. To Judas, Jesus will say one day in Gethsemane: "My friend. . ." But to Peter, to whom Jesus will entrust the care of his brothers, he says: "Get behind me, Satan!"

And yet, later he asks Peter: "Do you love me?"

It seems that the further someone is away from God, the more lovingly God approaches. Indeed, God is driven by only one motive, revealing the essence of his being, not because the person merits it – because, in fact, there is no merit – but because that person is in absolute need of God's loving attention.

Justice gives what a person deserves; mercy gives what a person needs. Such is the heart of God.

The New Testament often speaks of sinners. Of great sinners, too. Let us take a closer look at the encounter of such a person with Jesus. It is a woman, probably a sinner, maybe even a great sinner. Strangely enough, though, in the whole story this qualification never comes up – as though it was not important for Jesus. She is a human being, a human being in distress. And thus, she experiences the utmost attention from Jesus the Messiah. God gives his *communio*, his communion – building nearness first to those who most need it.

The external circumstances are important in this report that John passed on to us in the fourth chapter of his Gospel because they corresponded to what was happening internally. Here too, like so often in John's Gospel, he presents subtle, coherent details which show that he was an eyewitness. For that I am deeply grateful to him. The other evangelists were familiar with this scene as well; some might even have been present, but they did not regard it worth writing down. Maybe they did not dare to announce publicly what had been revealed in the protected space of non-believers, in a Samaritan village.

Jesus was at the well of Sychar in the midday heat. He had just been with his disciples at the Jordan river. His men had been baptizing – gaining even more popularity than John the Baptist with his followers – and that led to nervousness among the Pharisees. They wondered: "Is this yet a second movement outside the system?" That was too much! Jesus himself had not stood in the water and baptized. His method did not include baptizing with water. Later, when he sends out the disciples, we never hear him advise them to baptize. No, he says: "Heal the sick and proclaim the kingdom of God!" (Mt 10:7-8, Lk 9:2) For that, obviously, no baptism was needed.

Heal the sick? Proclaim the kingdom of God? Had not his men gained such great success *baptizing*?

Does not God's Holy Spirit sometimes allow the old and numerically strong to disappear, because he wants to bring about something new, still small in numbers, but closer to the original plan of God's kingdom?

We are not told which disciples were with Jesus. They are simply called "apostles." Was Judas among them? Judas seems to be the only one of the apostles who came from the south, from Kariōt, the desert to the southeast of Hebron. Would that make him something like an outsider, a stranger in the group of the disciples? Did he ever really feel at home among the men of Galilee? Did he ever feel at ease with the lake and the fish? He was different from the others by his origin and his mentality. What had brought him here to the north anyway? Or lured him here? That perhaps the Messiah had come? We don't know.

We are at the well with the group around Jesus. And now geography comes into the picture. The well is close to a crossing of two roads. They are age-old caravan paths – one linking Egypt with Syria, the other the Mediterranean Sea with Mesopotamia. The one road comes up from the Jordan valley in the east and runs straight west through the cross-roads to the ancient town of Sichem and over the head of the pass to Galilee. The pass divides Mount Ebal in the north from Mount Gerizim in the south. The second road comes from Jerusalem, from the south. Jacob's well lay a thousand feet north of where the two roads met. Another 330 feet north is the tomb of Jacob.

But there is yet a third road––the continuation of the one coming up from Jerusalem in the south. It curves slightly to the right leading down to Scythopolis (Beit She'an), into the pagan district of the Decapolis. Along this road, a little over half a mile north of the crossroads and the well, lay the village of Sychar.

Why the well is so far from the village is easily explained. A well was a desirable place for caravans to stop, but a caravan could not camp inside the village. (Even today the rest areas for trucks are outside cities). Therefore, in a wide arc around the well there were neither trees nor bushes.

It is there that Jesus sees a woman coming up the slightly curved road. She carries a water-jug on her head. It is noon and heat shimmers over the land. The woman is coming alone. That is not only unusual but also dangerous, because of wild animals and men. Women always went together in a group, as they still do today in Africa or in India. Her coming alone tells Jesus that she probably has a problem, a big one. She must have been excluded by the village. The other women don't want to be in her company. It is as though she is someone excommunicated, a heretic. Jesus notices too, that she comes in the heat of noon, uncommon in these latitudes. Women usually go to the well in the late afternoon. This is another sign that she is probably excluded, alone. He senses that her social loneliness is at the same time also a loneliness of her soul. She is a person who is suffering. She needs someone to be near to her. She needs communion.

A true pastor sees first a person's soul, not their sin or possible wrong behavior. He senses what might cause their suffering, what problems burden and weigh them down, preventing them from being free. He sees what his or her life needs now. Keep in mind that it is not about what a person deserves, but what a person needs.

Here too, he sees what the woman approaching needs.

But Jesus has a problem: his disciples! The way these men reason is deeply rooted in the Jewish legalistic thinking of their time. According to the Law, it is forbidden to speak to a woman, especially to a Gentile, someone outside Judaism. No, as long, as his men are around, he would not be able to speak openly with the woman. His disciples would feel an immediate disapproval and, from the start, would reproach wrongdoing. This created anything but a peaceful atmosphere of trust, in which she could open up in a pastoral conversation. I imagine that Jesus surely sensed that, and looked for a solution to provide a calm, peaceful space for a conversation. It was actually quite simple. He just had to arrange for the disciples not to stay around – and so he sent them into the village to buy food. . .

True, that is not written in the text. But I believe, John has described everything so clearly – in fact, he has also made us visualize the geography – because he wants us to see how carefully Jesus prepares a lifesaving yet difficult conversation.

Again, the way our Lord acts is a sign for us. Because such conversations with a person who is depressed can be difficult, it is important that he or she be given every advantage and that it is set up in such a way as to let that person feel at ease as much as possible. The law (in our days, not even Canon Law) should not be at the center, but the human person, a person in distress. It is that distress that draws Jesus close to her. His correctness in sending the disciples away became clear when they come back *astonished* that he was speaking to a woman. They took offense because their Master did not obey the instruction of the Torah.

That's how they were, putting the Law above the person.

With someone in psychological distress, you need to speak to them alone to gain trust. Trust? No, even before that, something else is essential to allow trust to develop: to make yourself likeable. Kindness is the necessary first step to gain trust. (I will not share anything personal with someone who is not likeable).

Therefore, to gain her trust Jesus must first gain her sympathy. *She* needs to find *him* likeable! Jesus accomplishes that in an instant, with one sentence (the sound of his voice and his regard for the woman undoubtedly contributes to making him likeable). What he does is awesome, exemplary, a sign of freedom.

"Dós moi peĩn." – *"Give me a drink."*

The Samaritans were most familiar with the Pentateuch, the first five books of the Bible. From the first of these, the book of *Bereshit* (in the beginning/Genesis), they knew the beautiful account of Abraham sending his senior servant to his homeland to bring home a wife for his son Isaac (Gn 24). Approaching the city of Nachor, after a long trip, the senior servant made his "camels kneel down outside the city by the well of water; it was towards evening, the time when women go out to draw water." And then he said to a beautiful young woman, Rebekah, "Please let me sip a little water from your jar" (Gn 24: 11, 17).

When the Samaritan woman heard the Jewish stranger say these words: "Give me a drink," the age-old words of the Scriptures might have naturally come to her mind. In Rebekah, one of the great matriarchal figures of Israel, she may have seen herself. Rebekah, too, had been addressed in this way – and marriage happened, *communio*, close communion, oneness.

What delight must have blossomed in this woman at the well to be addressed in this way. Her heart was glowing. But mixed with the delight there was also irritating surprise. This man was not allowed to speak to her like that, asking her for water!

As a man he was not allowed to speak to a woman, as a Jew he was not allowed to speak to a Samaritan. And to ask this woman for water, to drink out of her jug? Never! We may well say that Jesus, the Jew, is breaking rules and laws of his time to win a person for himself. He speaks from a religious sense that is not static but able to adapt in always new ways. This religiosity does not allow itself to be constrained by legal texts, but is penetrated by a relationship with an all-loving, merciful God. He gives the human person, the creation of God's hands, what he or she needs, not only what the law permits.

But precisely because Jesus is breaking the Law, he wins the sympathy of the woman. Why is that so? Does he sense, suspect, or even know that she too had frequent conflicts with the Law throughout her life, had gone against norms and broken the rules – and now meets a Jew who likewise is not too strict about rules and norms? It makes this stranger likeable. He is of her kind, a kindred soul.

To win someone's sympathy by making myself equal, by adapting to certain customs of theirs and joining in with them, even if I have to break rules in order to do so – that calls for great inner freedom and unconditional nearness to the person. Every form of therapy and pastoral care, especially the Church's, should always take Jesus' behavior as a model and be guided by it.

Ultimately, God already acted in this way with the incarnation of his Son. He has become like us in everything (even in sin: By the standard of the Torah, in his time Jesus was one of the greatest sinners. For this reason, he was put to death.) He has shared our life, including death. Is that not a wonderful God, "who, though he was in the form of God, did not regard equality with God something to be exploited, but emptied himself, taking the form of a slave, being born in human likeness, and being found in human form, he humbled himself and became obedient to the point of death, even death on a cross" (Phil 2: 6-8). That is why we can trust God. Through his life in lowliness, being in our midst, he has won our sympathy. God is not disturbed by our sins; he focuses neither on sin nor on laws, but on the human person who is the apple of his eye. His only concern is how to win each person over.

The woman – she had a name, perhaps Archela – is surprised and delighted, but probably also irritated. How can this man talk to her like that? Consulting the Greek text of the Gospel, the surprise still re-echoes in the words in which she now answers him:

How? You? A Jew? You ask me, a Samaritan woman, for something to drink?

If anyone would ask why the evangelist knows all these words with such certainty, even though he was not present, the answer is simple. After this encounter, we learn, the villagers invited Jesus and his disciples to their village and so John had plenty of time to ask the woman: "Listen, what was it that the two of you were talking about?"

Yes, what did they talk about? She remembers that he treated her like a normal woman. Just that alone was new and liberating, considering how she had been treated by the people in the village. She remembers that he told her profound words of wisdom, which she hardly understood, so mysterious and mystical were they: "If you knew the gift of God and who is saying to you, 'Give me a drink,' you would have asked him and he would have given you living water" (Jn 4:10).

"Living" water did in fact flow at the bottom of the well, fresh water from Mount Gerizim. So, this Jew knew that, but how did he intend to reach that water?

"'Sir, you have no bucket, and the well is deep. Where do you get that living water? Are you greater than our ancestor Jacob, who gave us the well, and with his sons and his flocks drank from it?'" The Bible does not tell us directly that Jacob dug this well or "gave" it to anyone. But in the book of Genesis (33:19), it is mentioned that Jacob bought a piece of land near Sichem, where he pitched his tent. According to excavations, this old Sichem (Tel Balata) lies just over a quarter mile west of Jacob's well. That does coincide with the biblical account. If a person who was a nomad in those times would buy a piece of land, there was no need to mention that he dug a well – without water he would not have been able to live there. The mention of the purchase of the land *is* the mention of the well, as we would presume today that a newly built apartment has a connection to the water main. The purchase of the land in exactly this place is a sure indication of the well. We have to think in the reverse. Through one of his people with special skills, as we have them still today, Jacob first had to find out whether there was water, and then he bought the plot and dug the well for his sons and his herds.[2]

In the wider region, Jacob's well is the only one with flowing water. It is deep, unimaginably deep. Its bottom had been located at a depth of sixty-two feet, but that was only an estimation based on the rocks people had thrown in there throughout the centuries to hear how deep it might be. In 1955, when Greek monks cleaned out the well, they encountered flowing water at a depth of 164 feet (!). We can only imagine how heavy the rope alone must have been to lower the bucket.

Coming back to the woman, judging by her words and the following conversation, we can conclude without a doubt that she knew how to speak, how to communicate with men without any shyness, and that she was familiar with Holy Scriptures and Tradition.[3] She obviously communicated with ease, and this ease might have turned disastrous for her in the course of her life – a nice conversation, which became longer and more intimate, developed into a relationship she had never had in mind – and without intending it, she found herself a prisoner of her own gifts. This happened many times, and now again? At this point in the conversation, she would have given no thought to that, and Jesus had something altogether different on his mind than an amorous adventure.

His answer is serious: "'Everyone who drinks of this water will be thirsty again, but those who drink of the water

---

2. Linked to this well is also the rape of a woman. Dinah is one of the daughters of Jacob. Rebekah and Dinah were at the same well with Jesus who wants to give his nearness, his communion, to everyone.

3. Her conversation with Jesus is similar in length to the one Martha will later have with Jesus at the tomb of Lazarus.

that I will give them will never be thirsty. The water that I will give will become in them a spring of water gushing up to eternal life" (Jn 4:13-14).

Jesus alludes to the woman's daily trips to the well, to the never-ending fatigue of carrying the water. But then he speaks of a different, peculiar water that will forever quench every thirst and make the tiring trip to the well unnecessary. Even more: this man himself will become a life-giving source for others, a source leading even to eternal life.

The stranger's mysterious words promise the woman something wonderful, never hoped for. They are spoken without asking anything in return, simply as a gift to her, given freely. She perceives that as an honor, an honor lasting into eternity. By turning to her in this way, without requiring conditions, such as repentance, conversion and penance, Jesus breaks through her loneliness and isolation. He makes her, the outcast, the recipient of his gift, and a source of life for others.

And yet the woman cannot understand all this at once.

"Sir, give me this water, so that I may never be thirsty or have to keep coming here to draw water" (Jn 4:15).

These words clearly show that Archela has not yet grasped the deep spiritual meaning of Jesus' mysterious words. How could she? She understands on the practical level. "Wouldn't it be wonderful if this stranger – maybe he is a *water diviner*? – could build a water conduit all the way to my house, so I don't have to come here every day carrying this heavy water jug. . . Yes, please, do that!"

Jesus realizes that his deep theological words are not understood by this woman. The same thing happens later on, when he tells his apostles: "You will drink the chalice. . ." or to the believers in the Synagogue in Capernaum, "Whoever eats my flesh and drinks my blood will have eternal life . . ." On those occasions, too, those listening to him do not understand what he means. They need time, reflection, and new experiences for that.

However, the conversation by now had come to a dead end. Jesus could not and would not build the water conduit. What then, we should ask, had been the goal of this conversation? He certainly wanted to grant this woman salvation, save her, and make her happy. But that meant especially healing what was broken, what was dark in her soul and in her past. With the method he had used so far, he had not reached this goal. All he had achieved was that she continued the conversation with him, listening with curiosity, and obvious liking this Jewish stranger.

Clearly, he had won her interest and her sympathy.

He was able to do that because he did not reproach her, did not say things, like for example, that she did not understand because she was too simple-minded. He did not blame her for not comprehending what he was saying but took the seeming failure upon himself. Besides, this is not about fault. The woman simply did not want anyone to touch what was so painful and had marked her for life. However, to be healed it is necessary to reveal one's inner wounds.

When at Mass we pray before communion: "Look not upon our sins . . ." something of a merit-based image of God does resonate, as if to say, "Because of our sins, we don't deserve any mercy from you." But do we tell a doctor, "Don't look at my wounds?" Do we tell God, the motherly Father, the savior of the whole world, "Don't look at my sin?" If not to God, to whom can we show *everything,* including all our sins, because he wants, and will, and can heal them! That is why in our heart we should pray: "Look at our sins!" Because all that God looks upon will be healed.

Jesus wants to look at what is sick in this woman's life and at what is tormenting her. He wants to do that with everyone.

That is why Jesus adapts and changes his methods, which takes delicacy and humility. You must realize and admit to not having said the right thing. Such a switch in method also contains a risk: you could lose the person you want to save.

Up to now Archela's former life did not matter. Jesus simply took this woman seriously, met her with kindness and loving attention, and showed her mysterious visions of the future which sparked her curiosity. A good and friendly relationship had come about. Is it sound enough to support what is difficult to face? What he now brings up?

"Go, call your husband, and come back."

The change of topic, fast and abrupt, touches exactly those areas of her life she wanted to hide. She is shocked, her wounds dare to break open again. But in Jesus' words neither does he condemn nor does he distance himself from her or banish her. On the contrary, it is as if he says: "Come back again!" She, who lives in a relationship with a man outside the divine law, is invited by the Son of God himself to approach, together with this man, the *communio*, the encounter with the Holy One.

We do not know how Jesus knew about the woman's problematic relationships. He could have guessed something from the circumstances, like how and when she has come to the well. But a prophet does see things that normal people do not see.

Her answer in its brevity says a lot: "*Ouk* échō àndra – I have no husband."

Up to this point she had been very articulate, but now utters only three words. She breaks up the communication, as though wanting to say: "I'm not going to talk about that. Leave that alone, that is *my* messed-up life." And most probably her psyche causes her to lower her head as she speaks these words; she *shuts down*, we say. For a moment it seems that she will break contact with Jesus. But the sympathy she has gained for him keeps her with him.

Jesus' reply is full of tender compassion. It is made of three parts. The first part is confirming, building up: "You are right in saying, 'I have no husband'. . ." The second brings facts to light: ". . .for you have had five husbands, and the one you have now is not your husband. . ." The third part is consoling, uplifting: "What you have said is true!" There is nothing condemning in his answer.

Jesus invites her to come to him, together with the man who by law is not her husband, to be in *communio* with the Son of God. Where Jesus is, there is Church.

The overall situation and John's way of describing the woman's behavior suggest that Archela's fate is not intended to resemble Sara's in the book of Tobit. Her seven husbands all died in the bridal chamber (Tob 6:14). It would neither fit the circumstances described here nor the words of Jesus. No, here we can only assume that she had been in some way married five times, in a way possible at that time, and was five times divorced, or rather separated, and now for the sixth time is living with another man, but not by the law. Maybe the villagers even considered her a prostitute.

However, according to today's standards she could be compared with a woman who was five times married and divorced. Leading up to this point Jesus has admitted her to *communio,* to closeness and unity with him, who is full of mercy, because he gives his nearness not by merit or because everything has been done correctly and according to the law, but by the distress of the person and her present need.

Someone whose ultimate reference is the law and the commandments could attack and condemn her: "You slut, your miserable life is your own fault," or "You don't deserve better," or "You are getting the just punishment for your loose life," or "Now you have to do penance and show repentance, and God might show you his mercy, and perhaps accept you again. . ."

Not so the true God, who wants and will save every person. Jesus knows: this woman needs me. She needs someone who confronts her with the facts of her life, so that the wounds inflicted upon her can be healed. She needs someone who does not leave her to break down amid the chaos of her life. Thus, he *wraps* her story in two heartening, almost tender phrases, "You answered well," (that is how it is in the Greek), and then after the facts, "What you have said is true." John's great word of truth resounds, which Jesus here speaks to a woman who by our standards is a great sinner and should not approach the sacraments. But Jesus himself is the sacrament, and he lets her come to him.

Archela senses that, according to this man's words, the dark and messed-up part in her life is embedded in something beautiful and true – like a bandage both encloses the wound and enables its healing. She is not chased away, and excluded, but is accepted.

What by human standards should have made God "angry," the true God now uses to draw closer to the human person and save her. Because that is his name, his being: *Jeshua* – God saves.

How happy and deeply touched the woman may have felt in reaction to the encounter with Jesus is left to the sensitive imagination of the reader. . .

According to the Gospel text, the woman then switches immediately to a new and different topic, a theological one, far from her personal problems.[4] It has been interpreted as an attempt on her part at *distraction*. I regard that interpre-

---

4.　"Sir, I see that you are a prophet. Our ancestors worshipped on this mountain, but you say that the place where people must worship is in Jerusalem" (Jn 4:19-20).

tation as totally out of place. The woman has no need to divert attention from anything, and Jesus precisely wants to heal her wounds, our wounds. No, she can now look at and voice without shame, all the darkness and guilt and burden in her life. This Jew won not only her sympathy, but also her trust. He knows everything, she is sure of that, but he does not condemn her. He accepts her, consoles her, with him she can let go of everything. He holds her in his arms. Always and forever.

We can assume that Jesus gave her time to verbalize everything so as to finally unburden herself. She could get rid of all the embarrassment and dishonesty, everything she had sought in her life – it was all gone. Finally. Forever. Yet he kept her with him, but this opening oneself to the other and holding the other belonged only to the two of them.

Whatever the woman told John about this conversation afterwards – this deeply personal part she did not share. And John too understood that all those details did not belong in the public character of the Gospel. I am convinced that the evangelists came to know many things firsthand from those involved. For instance, Luke must have heard from Mary, the Mother of Jesus, about the Annunciation and Jesus' birth. Luke and John heard about certain encounters directly from Mary Magdalene, who was from Bethany.

Let's return to the well. In the end, the woman took a deep and freeing breath. No burden lay on her any longer. She had wiped away the last tears then looked at this wonderful man who understood everything and she said: "I still have one question that I have had since my childhood. But I cannot ask anybody. Everyone laughs at me. You will not laugh at me, that's why I can ask you. . ." It is about the theological matter mentioned previously.

"Sir, I see that you are a prophet. Our ancestors worshipped on this mountain. . ." and she looked up to Mount

Gerizim ". . .but you say that the place where people must worship is in Jerusalem."

In our society today, you might ask more simply: "What is the true religion? Mine or yours?" This question has occupied our minds and agitated us in many and dramatic ways throughout this century. Many avoid it and say: "Oh, but we all believe in the same God. . ." That answer reveals indifference and demonstrates mental laziness and a lack of discussion. Indifference is the illness of our times. The alternative is not fundamentalism, because fundamentalism avoids sound reasoning and discussion. The alternative is to do what is good, what is love, what is mercy. That's where answers develop.

It becomes clear immediately that the woman could not pose this question, the deepest and most beautiful question of her life, to anyone. Had she asked one of her Samaritan priests, he probably would have given her a resounding slap in the face. How dare she question her religion! And had she asked a Jew he would have only laughed at her – she did not even need to wait for his answer.

No religion will say of itself that it is not the true one! But saying: "Our religion is the true one!" while it may be right, in most cases is not helpful.

Words are not helpful, only actions done out of love.

Every person carries in themselves deep, very deep questions. It is not uncommon that at the end of a retreat, a question is asked softly, sometimes even by older priests: "Does God really exist? Has Jesus truly risen? Is he really present in the Eucharist?" These are wonderful questions, and they can well be answered. Often these questions and doubts bring us ahead in our understanding. However, one must voice the questions and search out and find the person who can be of help in searching for an answer. That will always be a person who has won my sympathy, in whom I find knowledge, and whom I trust. It has to be a person I can trust not to take offense at my fundamental question, someone who won't laugh at me, but, on the contrary, will be happy about my asking and go with me in search of the answer to life.

The woman has this trust: "This Jew who knows so much, him I can ask, and he will not mind me asking the question. He will not laugh at me or pull out his learned tradition and repeat well-known phrases. No, he will tell me the truth." And that is exactly what Jesus does.

"Woman, believe me, the hour is coming when you will worship the Father neither on this mountain nor in Jerusalem" (Jn 4:21). Jesus addresses her with the original word of creation: "Woman." With this word he will address another woman crying uncontrollably at his feet, anointing them with oil and kissing them: "Do you see, Pharisee, this woman?" (It is Mary Magdalene). On the cross he will address his mother with these words: "Woman, behold, your son!" And here is this woman. It is as though Jesus does not want to make any distinction between saints and sinners. They are all created beings of the one Father, unique human beings. That is how God judges the world. He gives everyone the same attention, including those who have put themselves outside of the "law of God," (which all too often is the law of man), and therefore, (by human standards) don't deserve the grace and the nearness of God. Also, and *especially,* to those people God gives his nearness, his embracing care, yes, his respect: "Woman!"

He confirms her trust: "Yes, you can believe me." There is a reason for the woman's trust in Jesus. He did not want anything from her for himself, but he gave her something of himself, new life, God's loving attention. He is not asking anything in return. He does not condemn her despite all he knows about her and her life. Yes, he knows what others don't know.

And then he speaks of the "hour" that will come. Immediately afterwards he even says that the hour has already come . . . In Jewish tradition this is an allusion to the coming of the Messiah. "On that day: A pleasant vineyard, sing about it!" (Is 27:2). "The days are surely coming, says the Lord, when I will raise up for David a righteous Branch" (Jer 23:5). And now it is not only days; now the hour has come. This is one of many "hidden" messianic statements of Jesus, the Nazorean, descendant of David, about himself, understandable to Jewish ears.

What he says now about this "hour of the Messiah" is mind-boggling, overturning the system! "Woman, believe me, the hour is coming when you will worship the Father neither on this mountain nor in Jerusalem. . ." Such a phrase out of the mouth of a Jew is virtually unthinkable; it is utter blasphemy. Had his disciples been present they would have left him, saying: "'Forget him! This is too much!" Because if they are murmuring about him speaking to a woman, a Samaritan, then they would be totally alarmed at him questioning the temple in Jerusalem, Zion, from where instruction comes.

Why can Jesus tell this woman something he could never have told his disciples? Why is it that she is open to it, and the disciples are not?

As we have heard, along the course of her life, the woman had frequently broken the law, which was con-sidered God-given. She was, one could say, familiar with trespassing, with non-law-conforming behavior. That is why Jesus, this Jew, had gained her sympathy. And what he was saying now was once more outside the norm. It was terribly forbidden, but somehow beautiful. It spoke of freedom, truth, divine wisdom. . .

The disciples instead, we may presume, lived in the center of their faith, behind walls and laws that separated right from wrong. The more we live closed off in the center, the less receptive we are to the "new" that does not coincide with tradition. Those who live at the "margins" must deal with what is new daily, experience the vastness of the earth and of heaven and of humankind. Instead, those who stay in the safe, saturated center, most of all experience *themselves*, hearing from all sides the familiar, old thoughts.

Heaven is also behind walls, surely, but you see only a small part of it. . .

Active recognition needs both the center and the margins – the solid trunk, and the lively leaves at the tips of the branches. Jesus lived in the center *and* on the margins; he sat at table with sinners *and* with religious leaders; he called God his Father *and* broke the Sabbath; he was a Jew *and* loved the Gentiles – but it seems he could communicate more easily with Gentiles and sinners than with religious leaders.

The woman must have sensed something of this vastness in him, and it spoke to her. She was open and susceptible to this vastness. To her Jesus could speak the "new"; the disciples instead needed years to get there, like Peter, who rigorously refused to eat what was impure, even when it was offered to him three times from heaven. Only when he stood on the doorstep of the pagan centurion did he understand and step across the boundary (Acts 10). He broke the law for the greater love and broader vastness of heaven, which is shining over all, sinners as well as the devout, the bad and the good.

The woman, the sinner, was now a friend of this freedom and vastness of heaven. To this heaven, all have admittance.

It needs to be pointed out that Jesus does not say, "You will worship *God,*" but rather, "*the Father.*" God is characterized as someone who cares for his own, as does every good father. Blessed are those who have remembrance of such a father and carry him within their heart throughout their life. By speaking of God as father, Jesus gives God a *face*, and shows him as a relational being, in a giving relationship. God is not a *police officer*, but a motherly giver. Perhaps the woman needed such a father to erase the power of destructive memories of her own father (or mother?). Certainly, with these words Jesus reveals something very intimate of his own relationship with "the Father, whom only the Son knows."

To worship the Father. . . The Greek verb *proskynéō* means to *humbly adore*, worship. It is used nine times during Jesus' conversation with the woman, nine times in only five sentences, as often as nowhere else in the Gospels. The *magi*, too, searching for the newborn king in Jerusalem, came to *worship* him, to humbly adore.

In the Western world this form of showing respect seems to be almost completely lost. We move "at eye level" with everyone and give a friendly pat on the back to the other person. . . In many encounters this does have its justification, but – even though the thought seems strange to us today – in a few, well founded and self-decided cases, it could signify a loss, a loss of respect, of dignity and recognition. Notice how the Holy Father, Pope Francis, slightly bowed in front of every refugee with whom he shook hands. Some in his retinue may have considered that his gesture showed a loss of holiness, but in reality, it is an *expression* of holiness because the Holy God has respect for each person, for everyone, also for the stranger and the sinner. Jesus has respect and reverence, for this woman.

The following sentence seems to reprimand her, but only seemingly so: "You worship what you do not know; we worship what we know, for salvation is from the Jews" (Jn 4:22). I understand these words as a communication of facts. The historical path of God's promise, of his salvation for all people, did not pass and does not pass through the Samaritans, but through the Jews. Through the Jewish people, even though, much lamented by their prophets, they had to suffer due to their many failures throughout their history. But God remained faithful to the way he had chosen: "Salvation comes from the Jews." What a wonderful phrase! But these words also contain the fact that salvation is not *limited* to the Jews – just as the water that comes from this well is not limited to the well.

"But the hour is coming, and is now here, when the true worshippers will worship the Father in spirit and truth, for the Father seeks such as these to worship him. God is spirit, and those who worship him must worship in spirit and truth" (Jn 4:23-24).

Who does Jesus mean when he speaks of "true worshippers"? Then what should we call the opposite? Are they liars, deceivers or just deluding themselves? Or should those who "truly worship God" be separated from those who only pretend to worship God – while adoring only themselves, paying homage to self-made gods?

If we listen well, Jesus provides criteria for distinguishing the true worshippers. They are the ones who worship God "in Spirit and in truth." It could be that Jesus joins his great friend, Isaiah, who 700 years earlier had raged against superficial temple rituals: "What to me is the multitude of your sacrifices . . . I have had enough of burnt offerings of rams and the fat of fed beasts. . . I do not delight in the blood of bulls, or of lambs, or of goats . . . bringing offerings is futile; incense is an abomination to me. . . Wash yourselves;

make yourselves clean; remove the evil of your doing from before my eyes; cease to do evil, learn to do good; seek justice, rescue the oppressed" (Is 1:11-17). According to Isaiah the authenticity of the temple rituals is to be recognized by its "giving for one another," most of all for the poor.

Those who truly worship God, worship "in Spirit and in truth." What could that mean? Under spirit/*pneuma* we understand relationship, the giving-relationship that exists in the triune God – God is Spirit, God is giving-relationship – that is God's being. Mercy, love – these are notions of a giving relationship, of giving to one another. And truth? This is the truth concerning who God truly is and who the human person truly is for God. Jesus dismisses all the concepts about God and the human person by which people make them fit their own dimensions. The human person is and will remain the creation of this motherly Father, and God is the one who gives everything for each person, even himself, in order to save everyone.

"*To worship God in Spirit*" could mean to acknowledge him and glorify him in a giving relationship. Wherever people live in this way, worship happens, and the meaning of Creation is fulfilled. "*To worship God in truth*" could mean living in accord with Jesus who says of himself, "I am the way, the truth and the life" and "everyone who belongs to the truth, listens to my voice." Whoever puts the human person at the center, whoever gives to their neighbor what they need to live, that person is dwelling in the truth the Father brought into the world. At the end, Jesus gives a simple, extremely short, new commandment: "Love one another." Whoever acts accordingly, will worship God in Spirit and in truth.

You might well say that once again Jesus conducts a sort of temple cleansing with the woman. He casts out a false image of God, one rooted in an established way of thinking. He explains that God is not as you have thought of him up to now, or what you should think of him, or what you may have suffered. God is different, totally different! He loves you as you have become and as you are now, standing here before him and before me, with all your wounds and faults and sins, with all that turned out badly and all that turned out well, and with the good you have done. He simply loves *you*.

Totally. Without end.

The woman is standing there, without moving. Her heart is quivering. Her lips are shaking. Her mind cannot catch up. But her soul jubilates and at the same time is paralyzed.

That's it!

That is what she had always wished to hear and could never believe. That is what sets her soul free.

Jesus gives her time. He is happy because he can see how his words reach her. They saturate her life and sow seeds of joy, exceeding every joy known to her.

Then the woman can speak again. Softly, still trembling, she says: "I know that Messiah [sic!] is coming (who is called Christ). When he comes, he will proclaim all things to us. . ." (Jn 4:25). And I feel as though you have proclaimed everything, and said everything, and as though now I know everything. And yet I cannot fathom it, cannot describe it . . . But then, if that is the case, then – then who are you? Are you the one who . . .?

With these lines John, the evangelist, has conveyed to us a preciousness so hidden that it is often overlooked. In Greek the phrase is: "*hoti Messías erchetai*" – "that Messiah is coming." In Greek, there is no article. It does not say "that *the* Messiah is coming." This is the only place in the New Testament where the word Messiah is used without an article. To some translators it may have looked like a mistake, which they attributed to the inattentiveness of the evangelist.

But he was not inattentive!

On the contrary! He was very accurate.

He quoted precisely, in its original form, what the woman later told him in the village. We need to ask in which language the two of them talked to one another. Surely not in Greek. Then in Aramaic, or Samaritan? These two languages differ from one another, especially in theological terminology. For example, for the Jews "Christ" is "*ha mašiah,*" in Greek "*ho Messías.*" For the Samaritans it is "*Taeb*"/" the One who will return" – and they used this term without any article!

The evangelist adapted that, and contrary to Greek linguistic usage, here, and only here, left out the article because he wanted to convey that these words were spoken in the Samaritan language.

We are hearing the actual words as they were said. Everything happened as it is written here.

And what follows is the fulfillment of *communio.* A communion, a unity, so profound that a human being can hardly grasp it in all its depth: "I am he, the one who is speaking to you." God gives his *communio,* his unity, not because a person has earned it, but because the person needs it, and because God wants to give generously. Such is his being. To sinners more than to the righteous. "I have come to call not the righteous, but sinners" (Mt 9:13). In his letter to the Romans, Paul takes up this revelation, these words, and writes: "And those whom he predestined he also called; [He uses the same word as Matthew.] and those whom he called he also justified; and those whom he justified he also glorified" (Rm 8:30).

The woman who was five times married and separated is glorified, because God wants to give this gift to her!

But then there is something else. I am not sure whether the evangelist was aware of this, too, because what happens next is similar to what he wrote down so accurately in the encounter on the "road to Emmaus."

While Archela is still dumbfounded in blissful happiness, the men are coming back. Noise fills the place, ordinary chatter, also murmuring about what they are seeing, namely that their Master is speaking to a woman, and to such a woman. But there was something that kept them from saying out loud any hateful words. The woman, however, senses the aura of the presence of the "divine" being disturbed – and she runs away. Runs away without her water-jug! What she came for has lost its meaning, was not necessary anymore; her thirst was quenched. The spring had broken open in her.

Such things are for real. The gift of the spirit can fulfill the needs of nature, and quench them, at least for a time. Jesus' natural hunger, too, has passed, as he now tells his disciples, it has passed because of the event of the Spirit.[5]

Two years later, Cleopas and his friend will recognize the Master, the Risen One, at *"the manner,"* when he breaks the bread. And they will be aware that their hearts were burning when he explained to them the meaning of the Scriptures. The same has happened here: the woman's heart was burning, becoming more enflamed, while the stranger explained to her the meaning of her life. Everything was good. And just as later, the "Emmaus" disciples will run

---

5. "Meanwhile the disciples were urging him, 'Rabbi, eat something.' But he said to them, 'I have food to eat that you do not know about.' So the disciples said to one another, 'Surely no one has brought him something to eat?' Jesus said to them, 'My food is to do the will of him who sent me and to complete his work'" (Jn 4:31-34).

back, overcoming every natural tiredness, she runs back now, since her every thirst is quenched. The disciples ran back to their community, on which they had just turned their backs; the woman runs back to the village community that has excluded her. And she herself can now pass on *communio*, establish a connection to Jesus. She goes to the people and tells them: "Come and see a man who told me everything I have ever done!" That sounds like a public confession of sins. But for her what was sin has become grace, what was judgment has become union with God. Her sin has helped her to find her savior.

God will use everything for the human person to find him – and he will set each person's heart aflame.

Where *communio* happens, there is resurrection.

In Hades – or: through fire

John, the evangelist, allowed us to participate in the unique encounter between Jesus and the woman, one who in the eyes of her people in a "Gentile" village was considered a great sinner. It was an encounter that became *communion* – deep communion, unity. Would Judas have been there?

If Judas was among the group of disciples who returned from the village of Sychar to the well, he saw the Samaritan woman. And she saw him. What could they have guessed, or even understood about each other in this situation? She was freed from the burden of her life by the *communio* with the Holy One given to her. He, Judas, lived in the *communio* with the Holy One of God, but didn't take advantage of this gift in order to become aware of the instincts and impulses that were driving him subconsciously, and possibly leading him to sin. Or did he, at this point, not yet perceive his thoughts and intentions as being contrary to God?

How many people live *parallel* with God, or walk by churches daily without taking advantage of the nearness of the Holy and Merciful One to clear their soul and its instincts, to distinguish and discern, until the Spirit of God can truly influence them?

What happens with those who do not use their days to perceive the dark parts of their life and allow it to be transformed into light? Even those who in the last hour reject God? Will God then, as we have always been told, respect that person's freedom, which, after all, has been given by him, and let that person go to hell?

At the well in Sychar, we witnessed a very gentle, kind, healing Jesus, who accepts the sinner and transforms sin into salvation. We witnessed an event in all its historic reality, with many consistent details. But don't the pages of the Gospels also present a hugely different Jesus, one who announces destruction? Who threatens with hell? To a mindful reader of the Holy Scriptures, in many passages it must seem as though Jesus took the sharp ax of his friend John the Baptist (Lk 3:9) into his own hands, swinging it destructively so as to hurl unscrupulous egocentrics into the eternal fire of hell.

Let's take a closer look at some of the passages in which Jesus clearly speaks of "hell" (I will limit myself to what is helpful for this book).

One thing needs to be made clear from the start. Jesus never spoke about "hell" for a simple, obvious reason – because he did not speak English. Instead, he used three other terms of his time (and from his language): *Hades, Abyssus* or *Gehenna.*

First, *Hades.* The Greek word for the "netherworld" (in Hebrew "*sheol*") should not be translated as "hell" because, according to the thinking of the times, one could come back again from Hades (see Tob 13:2; Rev 1:18). After the Second Vatican Council, the Catholic Church in Germany has changed the wording of the Creed "descended into hell" to "descended into the world of the dead,"[6] which is the meaning of the Latin *ad infernos* and accurately references the Greek *eis haden.* From the "netherworld" there is a return then, as we read even in the Old Testament: "The Lord kills and brings to life, brings down to Sheol and raises up" (1 Sam 2:6). That

---

6. Translator's note: in German it is translated as "*Reich des Todes.*"

is precisely what the Risen Jesus has done with those in the netherworld. He has led them with him into his glory.

Instead from "hell," as it is usually defined, there is no return. Therefore, between "hell" and "Hades" or the "netherworld," there is a world of difference. Moreover, the two expressions convey altogether different images of God. On the one side God would be the one who pronounces a death penalty, terrible torments without end; on the other side he is the one who wants to save, even if "through fire." We will see what that means.

Second, *Abyssus.* The word means "abyss." In some version of the Bible it is translated as "hell," which is incorrect.

Third, *Gehenna.* This word derives from the Hebrew "*Ben Hinnom*" and means the valley of the "sons of Hinnom," which is mentioned various times in the Old Testament (see Jer 32:35). It stretches from west of Jerusalem around the city down to the lowest point in the south. In this valley, 600 years before Jesus, humans had been sacrificed to Baal in the fire. In Jesus' times, it served as the garbage dump and sewer for the 35,000 inhabitants of Jerusalem, plus 120,000 pilgrims on the Holy Days. From the hill, water trickled down and every kind of garbage was disposed of in this dreadful place. The gases of the dump ignited, so there were always little fires smoldering. Thus, references to the "fire that never dies down" and the "place where the worm doesn't die" – because without doubt all kind of animals crept around there, searching for anything edible in the dirt.

Where the Gospels mention *everlasting* fire, we need to consult the Greek. In Matthew, we mostly find the word "*aiōn*," from which the English word "eon" derives, meaning "a long time." The passage in Matthew's Gospel (13:39) "the harvest is at the end of the *aiōnos*," does not mean at the end of "eternity" (that would be nonsense), but "age" – therefore, "a long time." Thus, everywhere we read "everlasting" in English, we need to be attentive whether the Greek meant "a long time." And instead of "hell," we should rather use "Gehenna," to explain this word. ("Gehenna" later on did indeed come to signify "hell," with the very new meaning of "eternal damnation as punishment in never-ending torment." This is a notion for which in Jesus' time no word existed).

There is a second factor that we absolutely need to take into consideration. Most passages (in the translations) that mention hell and everlasting fire are found in the Gospel of Matthew. We need to ask ourselves why this is so one-sided, why he is the only one who used these terms? Why not all four Gospels? Indeed, did these words came from Jesus himself? The fewest words mentioning punishing judgment are found in Mark, and in the Gospel of John. Here, too, we need to ask how that can be explained.

The time and place in which these Gospels came into being provides the first clue. Most scripture scholars think that all of them were written after the year 70, when Jerusalem was destroyed by the four legions of the Roman general, Titus. According to these scholars, Mark wrote first, then in the mid-eighties Matthew and Luke, and later still John. In which area, in which community, under which circumstances did they develop? And who were these so-called "evangelists?" Research can offer only weak hypotheses and these scholars were aware that their hypotheses were not solid.

There is an ancient record, however, that offers more precise dating for the Gospels. A document from one of the first Christians (Bishop Papias of Hierapolis, around the year 100, quoted by Eusebius of Caesarea), provides the following details.

According to that document, the Gospel of Mark was dictated by Peter in Rome to his translator Mark, in the mid -40s, after his flight from Jerusalem. At the same time in Jerusalem, in my estimation (and according to Irenaeus of Lyon), the former tax collector, Levi-Matthew, began to write his Gospel using already existing writings, his personal experience, and reports from the communities. Around the beginning of the 50s, the former Gentile and physician, Luke, started writing his Gospel, probably in Antioch. Luke knew Mark and also Matthew, and probably used other written sources, too. He conducted interviews in the communities and visited Mary, the mother of Jesus, Mary Magdalene, Paul, and John, the disciple in the region of Ephesus. Luke wrote his Gospel for a Roman audience and therefore left out what was specifically Jewish. Lastly, maybe in the beginning of the 60s, the favorite disciple, John, wrote his Gospel, wherein he did not repeat a fourth time what the others had already said. He too probably wrote in Ephesus, a big multi-religious and multi-cultural city. He addressed a metropolitan audience with little connection to Judea and to the time of Jesus, an audience that struggled to "believe."

Should my assumption, which I believe to be surprisingly well sustained, prove to be true, we can conclude that only Matthew wrote as a Jew for Jews in Judea, probably even in Jerusalem, and precisely in Aramaic. This strong Jewish environment suggests that Jewish legalistic thinking and ideas could have been inserted into his Gospel. Jerusalem was the stronghold of the law-abiding. For this reason, such strong emphasis on the Mosaic Torah (which is not present in the other Gospels) and typically Jewish forms of speech could find their way into his Gospel.

Thus, there may be an initial, well-substantiated, historically sound reason why Matthew's Gospel with its talk of "hell," or rather *Gehenna* and eternal fire, is so different from the other Gospels. Do these speeches perhaps derive from the Jewish environment?

A second factor: research has long known of Jewish so-called apocalyptic eschatological literature. It emerged in Palestine over many centuries, and was still present in Jesus' century, mostly among the Essenes. Circulating in Israel, it greatly influenced religious thinking. This literary genre contemplated and even predicted in multiple and strongly speculative ways, difficult to comprehend for us today, the end of the world and all that will happen when it comes.

At the center of these *visions* of the end of the world were ideas and sometimes bizarre sketches of the "judgment," the *krisis*. They mostly concurred with the belief that all Gentiles, who did not observe the Torah, as well as all sinners, would go into *Gehenna*. These Gentiles and sinners had to be transported into *Gehenna* first, and only thereafter the Messiah, or the new kingdom, would come for Israel.

In these eschatological circles and its literature, we regularly encounter the expression: "will be thrown into the outer darkness/into the furnace of fire; there will be weeping and gnashing of teeth." These expressions are found six times in Matthew (8:12; 13:42; 13:50; 22:13; 24:51; 25:30) and only in his Gospel, except for one parallel mention in Luke 13:28. These versions confirm a rich spoken use of this form of speech in the Jewish environment of the time.

We must wonder whether it is Jesus himself or Matthew who is speaking here about the "last judgment" and "hell," or how this form of speech, used in Jewish apocalyptic circles, found its way into Matthew's Gospel.

It could be possible that Jesus uses this language for his Jewish audience since it was a quite common expression, but he used it to achieve an altogether different goal. For instance, in Matthew 8:12, it is not Gentiles or sinners who are consigned to the furnace, but rather the "heirs of the kingdom." Thus, Jesus turns common thinking upside down.

In at least two essential points the Jewish Jesus differs in principle from these apocalyptic eschatological understandings.

1. He does not send sinners into *Gehenna*, but he calls sinners to follow him! He freely gives them salvation, allows them to touch the Holy One. Through a healing encounter, he transforms them and promises them Paradise! (The next stage necessary for a person's profound transformation – if not possible through the person themselves, then ultimately through God's own doing – shall be further explained below.) He does not judge according to what a person would *deserve* (according to the law), but according to what a person *needs*. That is mercy.

An unheard-of novelty, an outright radical counter-idea to everything that was said, taught and believed in his times.

The woman at the well in Sychar experienced this novelty. Will Judas experience it too?

2. Research discovered something else that is totally new in contrast with all the eschatological-apocalyptic Jewish descriptions of the day of judgement – Jesus alone brings a fundamentally new model. For him there is no need for all Gentiles and sinners to first disappear from the world so that the new kingdom can come about. Instead, he says: "The kingdom of God is among you!" (Lk 17:21). Amid the old, pagan, unbelieving, sinful world of violence, amid a world of suffering and death, the kingdom of God is already here and grows like a tiny seed.

Someone who thinks and acts so fundamentally differently cannot possibly have deliberately proclaimed such sentences of judgment with eternal fire as his own message. Either Jesus has appropriated common phrases or used such metaphors for another goal. For example, in Mt 8:12, those whom you never expected to be admitted to the heavenly banquet are precisely those who will enter into the kingdom of heaven – but you who have already written heaven into your calendar, you are thrown out into the fiery furnace! Or perhaps he himself did not use these expressions at all, and yes, perhaps some *law-abiding* person wrote them into Matthew's Gospel at a later date.[7]

Obviously, that does not explain all the passages about judgment, and this is not even the intention of this book. It is enough to say here that the most furious statements about "hell" and "eternal fire," in the way we read them today, cannot possibly stem from Jesus himself (and hardly from Matthew) nor are they meant to be understood in that way.

Reflect on Jesus' call to love one's enemies: "Love your enemies and pray for those who persecute you" (Mt 5:44). This means far more than simply enduring or forgiving! Jesus' mandate to love our enemies is enough to overturn, or even recognize as altogether impossible, the conviction of those who believe that the words about "hell" are from Jesus himself.

There are other passages in which Jesus speaks of "hell" (according to the mistranslation). How are these words to be understood? Here are some examples. We read: "Woe to you, Chorazin! Woe to you, Bethsaida!" (Towns along the sea of Gennesaret where Jesus had worked miracles). "[O]n the day of judgment it will be more tolerable for Tyre and Sidon [where Jesus was not active] than for you. And for you, Capernaum . . .you will be brought down to Hades" (Mt 11:20-24). And in another place, to escape the terrible

---

7. Probably also Mt 13:41-42; 22,13-14, as I have explained in my book: *Sentire Jesum – Jesus erspüren*, Paderborn 2014. (available only in German)

anguish, "it is better for you," Jesus says, "to lose one of your members than for your whole body to be thrown into hell"[8] (Mt 5:29) . . .

Altogether frightening because of the implied exclusion is the sound of this sentence: "For many are called, but few are chosen" (Mt 22:14). The Samaritan woman was not called, yet chosen and glorified! And Judas? Was he *only* called? Did Jesus ever distinguish between "calling" and "choosing"? Or did this expression, too, belong to a form of rigid law-abiding Judaism that excluded many?

Those chosen by Jesus would have been brought together from every corner of the world – how would the bad ones have escaped "the punishment of hell [*Gehenna*]" (Mt 23:33)? Therefore, everyone is admonished to be vigilant!

Jesus' harshest sounding words of condemnation are found in the parable of the "last judgment" when he says: "You that are accursed, depart from me into the eternal [*aiōnion*] fire prepared for the devil and his angels . . . And these will go away into eternal [*aiōnion*] punishment" (Mt 25:41-46).

Let us take a quick side glance at the evangelist John. The words he uses for the judgment sound significantly different. He says: "Those who have done good" will come out of their tombs "to the resurrection of life, "and those who practiced the evil things" will go "to a rising again of judgment" (Jn 5:29 YLT); "Those who believe in him [the son] are not condemned, but those who do not believe are condemned already, because they have not believed in the

---

8. As in other passages from Matthew's Gospel, Jesus' use of "hell" reflects how he is using the word as a metaphor for another goal, in this case to emphasize the importance of virtuous action even at great personal cost.

name of the only son of God" (Jn 3:18). And then again Jesus says: "For God did not send his Son into the world to condemn the world, but in order that the world might be saved through him" (Jn 3:17).

Therefore, God's judgment – his justice – ultimately consists in saving and in his mercy, which gives to the person, to sinners, what they need – not what they deserve! In this judgment much that is unpleasant and painful might come up – in fact, *needs* to come up – and ultimately be embraced, cleansed, transformed, and renewed by the great merciful One himself. Because in the fulfillment at the end of time, he will make "all things new" (Rev 21:5). All things!

Lastly Jesus' riddle: (Jn 9:39): "I came into this world for judgment, so that those who do not see may see, and those who do see may become blind." Jesus announces a wonderful judgment to us here. Once more he turns the religious leaders' thinking upside down! In the judgment, which means that Jesus is present himself, the blind (regarded as punished by God with blindness) shall regain their sight. This means, however, that their sin, be it only accredited to them or actual sin, will be taken away! Vice versa, those who are sighted, who believe themselves to be without sin, will become blind, sinners far from God. If thus they belong to the category of "blind ones," then – through this "detour" – they too will become sighted! With that, their sin too is taken away in the second step. Because ultimately God does not leave anyone in darkness and sin. Jesus explicitly calls the sinners who are far from God, like the Samaritan woman, and saves all who are in need of mercy.

In his farewell speech, Jesus speaks of "judgment, because the ruler of this world has been condemned" (Jn 16:11). If *this world* is marked by the ego, the "I" of the person, then it is judged by the You of God – judged in the sense of overcome.

Let us leave all threatening words be and let's take them seriously, even though they don't seem to match the kindness in Jesus' actions towards the Samaritan woman. They must have a good reason. We just need to find it.

We always have to understand the sense and meaning of a word in its particular cultural and temporal setting. Thus Mark, for instance, preserved one of Jesus' words against Peter, stronger than even what was said to Judas: "Get behind me, Satan. For you are setting your mind not on divine things, but on human things" (Mk 8:33)! According to these words of Jesus, to think of God as a human person seems to be a "satanic" sin. Here we see how the word "Satan" could be used metaphorically at the time, to characterize something, or someone, as terrible beyond words.

To conclude, let's take another verse from the Old Testament, in the Psalms: "...Before the Lord, for he is coming, for he is coming to judge the earth. He will judge the world with righteousness, and the peoples with his truth" (Ps 96:13). God's judgment here is understood as his truth. The New Testament cannot fall short of that.

This might be enough of a selection. Research counts many more of Jesus' words as belonging to his "judgment speech." It is said that the words about judgment provide the necessary seriousness of God's sovereignty, which ultimately, they reveal. And which I want to retain too. But what does this necessary seriousness consist in?

The serious meaning of Jesus' threatening words consists in a warning: "Don't do that!" "Be careful of that!" "Think ahead!" "Don't be lazy, otherwise . . .!"

The connection is not hard to see. If a person loves someone, and sees this person running into danger, he or she will warn them, so that no harm will come to them. Sometimes we scream spontaneously to warn another person. Not warning the other is a sign that I don't really care about them.

All of Jesus' words, in which he threatens us with "eternal fire" or "*Gehenna*" or similar things, and which are truly his own words, are to be understood as a warning, not as a damnation that will literally happen. This is not surprising considering that God is Love, and so he wants and will save those he created. How could he not warn them, so that they do not have to endure greater suffering than what they must already endure now?

Warnings are familiar to us human beings (they exist, of course, also among animals.) What would our cities look like if we did not have traffic signs? Everything would break down. We also find warnings on most packaging – with all kind of possible dangers listed, like for medications. We are even warned not to dry the beloved cat in the microwave.

No doubt, without warnings humans would not survive. Not to warn, in many cases would not only be uncharitable, but extremely negligent, and so under certain circumstances severely punishable.

But a true warning also has another element. The consequences of our actions that we are warned about, as well as the punishment involved, need to really happen if the warning is not heeded. The speed trap is effective only because we know that we will get a ticket if we exceed the speed limit.

Some warnings concern all of humanity, such as global warming, the pollution of our oceans, or the amassing of chemical weapons. If we continue to live like this, egoistically and in luxury, if we continue to throw away without concern for those who come after us, they will be the ones to pay the consequences. Warnings are intended to save. Too often we have a hard time learning something when things are going well. . .

Let's return to the Bible.

Just think what sense Jesus' parable of the "foolish virgins" would have if the "foolish" virgins were granted entrance into the wedding hall just like the prudent virgins. . . The parable would lose all its meaning; its message would have turned into the opposite: "It doesn't matter whether you act in the right or the wrong way. . ." It would be somewhat like a deflated balloon, its knot untied. The knot is necessary! It is necessary for branding the alternative as being wrong.

Or think of the harsh parable Jesus tells, in which the sheep to his right, meaning the righteous ones, can take possession of the kingdom of God. Should those on the left who did not do the works of mercy have entered as well? If people's actions were indifferent in front of God, Jesus would not have needed to share this parable.

It is, therefore, a necessary part of the narrative structure as well as the logic of the parables that those who did the right thing get rewarded, and those who acted in the wrong way get punished. Otherwise, the parable would have no message.

Now there is at least one parable in which Jesus states that in front of God a person's behavior is not the decisive factor, that – strangely enough – even the one who has acted wrongly is rewarded. That is the parable of the workers in the vineyard (Mt 20:1-16). In it the one who worked the least (and Jesus hints that the guy has been idle) receives just as much as the one who has been slogging away the longest.[9] How should we understand that?

In Jesus' parables we need to begin by considering the message that the Lord wants to tell us. Does he want to say something about us human beings, how we should act? Or is the message about God and his kingdom, about the attitude shown? Secondly, we need to consider to whom Jesus is addressing the parable.

Even though in the parable of the "workers in the vineyard," Jesus' interlocutors are not mentioned explicitly, they can be detected in a *hidden* way in the phrase that is the theme in various parables: "But many who are first will be last, and the last will be first" (Mt 19:30; 20:16). Because one thing is for sure: by his actual behavior Jesus has condemned no one. On the contrary, he was always intent on saving. The sinners, the needy, the last ones being first. . . and obviously, even though last, those who were supposed to be first, the righteous ones.

The parable of the "Last Judgment" (Mt 25:31-46), which Matthew passed on to us and which I believe largely leads back to Jesus himself, leads to the following conclusion: The primary message is positive. Those who "have done what is good," the seven works of mercy, whatever culture or religion they belong to, whether they believe in God or not, have done the right thing "before God." They have done what gives meaning and a goal to every life.

---

9. With this parable one needs to be aware that the sentence "because many are called, but few are chosen," added at the end of some accounts, does not fit into the parable as it is told. Perhaps here too the law-abiding Jews of the time are protesting God's goodness.

The example of the opposite, of those who do not do this, belongs to the Semitic storytelling structure and art which readily plays with opposite words and images. However, it does not carry any new message of its own, but provides a *negative* background, which can also be understood as a warning that underlines the positive message even more.

The word-images of the "undying fire for the devil and his angels" as metaphorical forms of speech derive from Jewish apocalyptic circles and were commonly used. For "heaven" or "paradise" or the "kingdom of God," of which the good ones will take possession, Jesus does not use any metaphorical description. As though their beauty and beatitude were inexpressible beyond all words.

A metaphor never intends a word in its primary meaning, but rather, uses it figuratively. Like: "That person is a fiery speaker!" No one in our culture will imagine a speaker in flames or a person spitting fire, but we understand this image as metaphorical, in the sense that if this person speaks, it is like fire, he enflames his audience . . . metaphorically! In the same way the words of the everlasting fire are intended metaphorically; they want to say that this is not the right way to act before God, and therefore, it would not be right for a human being to act in this way, it is not the way that leads to a fulfilled life. Thus, as a word-image, it intends to be a warning. A serious one!

By the way, also the phrase "last judgment" (which does not appear at all in the text) is to be understood metaphorically. Jesus does not want to describe how the last day on this earth will proceed. Aided by the eschatological awaiting of the last coming of the Son of Man at the "end of time," he wants to say what ultimately is the only important thing before God, what will be decisive in our life. Indeed, today, in the here and now, for every person, *in the end* it is a question of giving to others at the right time what they need in order to live. The metaphors about fire are only the framework to emphasize the seriousness of what is being said.

Let's recap then. Jesus did not condemn anyone. He came to save because he loves us. And because he loves us, he warns us. The threatening sound of his words stems from the Semitic culture of his time and is to be understood in a metaphorical way (and some of them are not *his* words), but their intention is serious. They want to say:" Think!" "Live differently, live the YOU," be the "I for you," which alone makes sense and gives meaning to life in this world.

It is always to be the YOU of God.

But Jesus did warn!

So, we need to pose the question: what did he warn us about? There needs to be something *looming*, something painful if we do not heed his warning.

In his first letter to the Corinthians, Paul wrote the expression which gave this chapter its title: as through fire, or as it is translated, "with fire" (1 Cor 3:11-15). Three times in this passage, he writes about *fire*. They are about the following:

Paul calls himself the builder who laid the foundation for the community in Corinth; another will continue to build. And yet how will the other continue to build? With gold or straw . . . (word-images which we immediately recognize as metaphors). It is up to each one, "the Day will disclose it, because it will be revealed with fire. And the fire will test what sort of work each has done . . . if the work is burned, the builder will suffer loss; the builder will be saved, but only as through fire."

Two statements stand out for us: fire brings to light, it tests, it purifies, and the *goal* is the *salvation* of the human person.

In our world, so controlled by technology and chemistry, many processes use fire: from pasteurizing milk to galvanizing steel, from spot welding to launching rockets, and thousands of others. Two thousand years ago, fire was used to purify many metals, most of all gold. The goal in this was not destruction but achieving a precious metal free of impurities. Though the techniques have been refined, even to this day, the method has not changed.

Fire, however, does not only purify, it also hurts. If you burn a finger with a match, you quickly pull back your hand. Many procedures in hospitals and doctors' offices (oh, the poor dentists and their patients!), but also in top-level sports, are not without pain. But the goal is always improvement. Pain is physical, but also spiritual, emotional; depression, too, is pain. For some, even psychotherapy is pain, because it uncovers behavior patterns that have always been pushed out of awareness and that a patient doesn't want to face. No one wants to face the fact that they act like a bullying good-for-nothing – because that means having to change their lifestyle!

"As through fire. . ." Now the metaphorical meaning of this phrase becomes clearer. It expresses a painful cleansing, but for a good goal, for a better state than before.

This raises the last question: what painful suffering did Jesus warn us about (precisely because he loves us and wants to spare us from this *hellish* agony)? What kind of *purification* is this about?

We have come to know, at the deepest core of our faith, that God is Love. Love means *to give of oneself, to become a gift for another*. In the triune God there is total giving of self, from the Father to the Son, from the Son back to the Father, and this giving of self is the Holy Spirit, who is the very relationship of Love in God. And what God is in himself, is also towards everything outside of himself (even though we cannot speak of *within* and *outside* of God). God gives of himself to creation like the sun gives its rays to the earth and all the planets.

God has embedded this principle of his innermost being in creation. Everything alive lives from receiving and giving. When people confine themselves to their own ego, want to have things their own way, set themselves above everything else, egoism rules – and that leads the living organism to wither. In the human community, too.

Jesus admonishes us to live the YOU of God.

Judgment means, therefore, that when we will stand before the face of God, we will stand before the absolute YOU, before infinite love. Before God there is no more deception. I recognize both God, as God is in truth, as well as myself, in the way I was and acted in my life. And I will discover in myself more or less numerous egoisms – and will no longer be able to shift responsibility for them to someone else. I will see where I have been guilty.

The more a person has lived the YOU of God in his or her life and has aimed for this love, the less change is necessary to enter into the boundless glory of God's love. But the more egoisms there are in a person's life, the more change, the more cleansing will be necessary – "as through fire!"

The tradition of the Church has called this process "purgatory," a place or a phase of cleansing (the word "purgatory" is metaphorically rich).

Since before the face of God everything will be of infinite greatness and clarity (as much as we can say with our limited understanding), also the knowledge of God will be of infinite clarity and beauty – and therefore, the attraction God will have for the person will be of infinite intensity. But at the same time, every person will recognize themselves, and that too, with a clarity as never before. This frightening self-awareness in relation to the infinite attraction to God's beauty will cause a pain that threatens to tear a person apart, agony that can neither be experienced nor imagined here on earth, since here we don't have the experience of infinity and clarity.

God does want to save. Everyone. "Purgatory/place of purification," "Hades/netherworld," is not the end of life, but the beginning of transformation. For the God of life, our life does not end at the threshold of human death. He who himself is unending life, continues *on the other side*. As Paul unequivocally states, the point is that the human person "will be saved" (1Cor 3:15). We find the same message also in 1 Corinthians 5:5. Here we read about the first case of sexual offense, and Paul hands the person in question over to "Satan for the destruction of the flesh, so that his spirit might be saved on the day of the Lord." Or in 1 Timothy 1:20, Paul hands over two men "to Satan, so that they may learn not to blaspheme." The goal, therefore, is never "destruction," but rather, judgment means salvation, even if it occurs through punishment, or "as through fire. . ."

Opinions differ on the notion of purgatory. While for some purgatory is self-evident as part of the handed-down deposit of faith, others no longer find any meaning in it. Therefore, I tried to find a better term to explain it, one that contains not only purging and renewal, but also necessary pain.

How about "rehab"?

Most surgeries a person undergoes aim at healing something, at healing the person. After the surgery, the person should feel better than before. Orthopedic surgeries often foresee and require a subsequent rehab. Already in the hospital, physical therapists have the patient make the first movements or take the first steps. These naturally are

painful, sometimes very painful. One feels exhausted afterwards, wants to leave and not carry on. And yet, continuing
the therapy, even though it is painful, is good and necessary
for healing to occur. That is even more so the case in the following weeks of rehab. Seeing the other patients with their
handicaps, on their crutches and walkers, with bandages
and splints, the patient might congratulate himself for being
able to move a few toes without pain. Then he has to follow
the exercises, many times a day, and not every therapist is
pleasant and kind. Here comes the groaning, the slow crawling, pushing oneself forward. And everything hurts, every
movement. . . How attractive the elevator that goes up to
the recreation room – but in purgatory there are no eleva-
tors, no painkillers, no sleeping pills, only steps, staircases,
perseverance. . .

Then there is something else especially important:
rehabs are geared predominantly to physical healing and
improvement. But a person is more than a body. The soul
also needs healing, needs rehab. It is relatively easy to say:
if you would have taken care of yourself in your youth, or if
you would have eaten less, had been more physically active,
had led a healthier lifestyle, had renounced certain things,
had not taken on so many risks. . . and so forth, you would
have avoided this outcome. With the soul there are a hundred times more "If only I would have. . ." Not always, but
often illness is the consequence of an unhealthy or egocentric lifestyle. This is even more so for the soul and its abysses.
Those, too, are treated in the heavenly rehab – with the goal
of healing.

If in the past we spoke of "purgatory" – the older ones
among us are used to that term – the emphasis was more
on pain and suffering, long and terrible agony, even if one
would eventually be released. With the image of a "heavenly
rehab" the emphasis is on healing, renewal – always through
pain. "Through fire" is not that inaccurate.

At the end of this book, I will say something about Jesus' well-known parable of the "rich glutton and the poor Lazarus." In it, I will show what an extraordinary revelation Jesus makes there to humanity, a revelation that nowadays we mostly or even totally overlook.

It is a parable about "heavenly rehab."

But this parable also gives a decisive clarification: The rich glutton could have saved himself from pain, incredible pain, if already in his daily life, on countless occasions he would have lived love – being for the other. A giving relationship is how we could describe the "kingdom of God."

That is the goal of "heavenly rehab."

Because this is what it depends on, this will be the fulfillment of the renewal that God had in mind from the beginning. God intends that the human person, the creation of *God's* love, will be transformed into this love. Out of their many egoisms, they allow themselves to be created anew into being the YOU of God, because God is love.

Human beings, learn to love!

Jesus' parables
of the three "lost ones"

Luke, and only Luke, in the center of his Gospel, in the fifteenth chapter, gives us a triple precious gift, the uniqueness of which is rarely recognized – three parables of "lost ones." The best known of these is the parable of the "lost [or prodigal] son," or as we tend to say today, of the "merciful Father." But both titles capture only marginally the deep meaning of what Jesus tells us here. Besides, to be precise, we should speak of the parable of *two* lost sons, because the second, the older one who doesn't want to go in for the festivities, seems to be more "lost" than the one who returns from being "totally lost." But we will get to that later.

In the previous chapter, I pointed out that in order for Jesus' parables to be understood properly, two fundamental things need to be kept in mind. First, we need to ask ourselves to whom Jesus addresses the parable and what are the questions or convictions of the respective audience? Second, we need to ask ourselves: in the parable, does Jesus describe how human beings should deal with each other and how they should lead their lives, or does he want to share with us how God acts towards us?

Therefore, to begin with, let us look at the background of this wonderful triple parable and ask: To whom does Jesus address it? What are the convictions that shaped these men?

We have two groups of people drawing near to Jesus, with opposite opinions and intentions. First there are tax collectors and sinners, and second, the Pharisees and scribes.

The wording "tax collectors and sinners" is a little odd, because tax collectors are sinners too, just one profession among the number of *sinful* professions. One could say therefore, "tax collectors and *other* sinners . . ." In 7:34 Luke mentions these two categories of people, "tax collectors and sinners" – and immediately afterwards he speaks of a woman who comes to the house of Simon the Pharisee to anoint and kiss Jesus' feet. She is called a "sinner," but from what is described one can deduce that this woman formally had been a *hetaera*, (something like an upscale prostitute). I share the understanding that it is Mary Magdalene. In Mt 21:31 Jesus says clearly: "the tax collectors and the prostitutes are going into the kingdom of God ahead of you . . ." He is addressing the high priest and the elders of the people, so more or less the same group of religious leaders that also we encounter in the beginning of the parable of the three "lost ones."

By default, tax collectors fell into the category of *greatest sinners*. Because of their profession, they could not keep the instructions of the Torah; and by collecting taxes, they needed to work with the Romans, the hated occupying power. In the Jewish rebellion against the Romans in the year 66, the tax collectors were the first ones to be killed by the Jews. The *pornai* [prostitutes] were regarded as equally worthless. They all were considered the worst sinners. The first book of Maccabees (14:14) says this about these sinners: "He [the hero Simeon] . . . did away with all the renegades and outlaws." That corresponds exactly to what we know from the eschatological-apocalyptic Jewish literature.

Such sinners are now coming to Jesus. According to common Judaic understanding, and well founded in Sacred Scripture, they ought to be thrown into *Gehenna*. Jesus should send them away. They do not have any business being alongside a man of God, otherwise the dirt of their sins could rub off on him, the so-called prophet, and he would become a sinner himself. That was the reasoning.

But of these people it is said that "they wanted to hear Jesus." This the most beautiful desire there can be, that people open their hearts and minds because they want to understand and take in what Jesus says and does! The Samaritan woman was one of them. I believe that in the coming decades our Church will work more, yes, even mostly, with people who truly want "to hear Jesus," who deeply want it – and don't just tag along out of sheer habit. Where people truly desire it, where people search for Jesus, working together becomes a great pleasure; it sets free a new vigor and leads to results which bear fruit that will last.

Opposing the sinners stands the group of the scribes and Pharisees who strictly observe the Torah. Their precise compliance with the Mosaic Law makes them clean. They are convinced that before God they are counted as just and therefore will enter heaven. They earned it. According to their image of God, which is *merit-based*, it is absurd and impossible that God should deal with sinners, people who have not "deserved" heaven. This Jesus who claims to be a man of God, he even *eats with them*! And so, they grumble.

The Greek word for "grumble" (*diagoggyzō*) is used only by Luke, in this particular passage, and then again in Jesus' encounter with Zacchaeus, the chief tax collector in Jericho – again a tax collector! (Lk 19:7). There we have the crowd of followers and parasites around Jesus who "grumble." In both passages the Greek term indicates a *strong* grumbling.

An even stronger expression is being "indignant" (*aganaktéō*): The other ten apostles, for instance, are "indignant" at John and James wanting to assure the best places for themselves (Mk 10:35). Equally "indignant" are the high priests and scribes when they hear the children shout: "Hosanna to the son of David!" (Mt 21: 15) at Jesus' entrance into Jerusalem. But Jesus too is "indignant" when his disciples turn away the parents with their children. In Luke, the head of the synagogue is also described as "indignant" (Lk 13:14), because the crippled woman lets herself be healed on the Sabbath, which is against the Torah of Moses.

Matthew uses an even stronger verb about the Pharisees who see that Jesus does not keep the purification laws – *eskandalísthēsan*. They perceive it as a scandal. Matthew uses this word fourteen times! Mark, Luke, and John combined use it another twelve times. For a nation as religious as Israel, Jesus was a scandal! The next step after an accusation of "scandal" could have been stoning.

This "man of scandal" not only broke the purification laws, but even sat down at table with sinners and ate with them! Among nomads and semi-nomads in the Semitic environment, to eat with someone, to share a meal, signifies unity and friendship. During my many pilgrimage retreats in Israel, I had the rare fortune of being invited by such half-nomads from three different family clans. To drink hot sweet tea with them in their tent, or strong coffee, or even to dip the hand in the same dish, creates a sense of belonging – "You belong to us now!" When Jesus is with these people, such behavior creates the highest sign of unity possible in this culture. The man of God gives his unity to the "worst of the worst" on earth, to the tax collectors and prostitutes.

What a totally different image of God, compared to that of the Pharisees, do we have in Jesus, who is the likeness of the Father! He is the founding figure of our faith, against whom all Christians, indeed the entire Church, need to measure themselves. His image of God is our measure and norm and duty.

God does not consider what you deserve. Because God, the motherly Father, is Love. God wants to give, give first and foremost to those who no longer expect the Most High, the Eternal, even to notice them.

We cannot really understand the New Testament without paying attention to the differing images of God that lie beneath the actions and words of the scribes and Pharisees, and Jesus' actions and words. Jesus frees and releases us from erroneous, humanly conceived images of God! But they do prevail, whether hidden or openly, in our faith even today.

Now it becomes clear to whom Jesus wants to reveal something. He wants to say and show the strict people of the law that God, who is merciful, does not turn first towards those who have deserved it by correctly fulfilling the law, but to those, who, while not having deserved anything, do need him. That is why Jesus *eats* with sinners.

Let us look then at the three parables.

In Luke's Gospel, we find first the parable of the lost sheep, second, the one of the lost coin, and third the well-known parable of the lost son; combined with it is the one of his brother, the second son, who does not want to go inside and join the feast.

I offered the parable of the lost son for reflection during a retreat many years ago. I will never forget a young mother who suddenly had tears streaming down her cheeks, sobbing quietly: "And what does God do if the daughter doesn't return?" There I was with my fine theology and yet I could not answer the simplest of all human questions. Since that hour I have asked that parable, have asked Jesus over and over, for years: "What do you do, if . . .?" And one day, heaven gave me the answer, loud and clear. An answer so beautiful and consoling that any human being, any mother, could only wish for it.

I don't know why Luke arranged the parables in this sequence. Did he put the story of the lost son at the end because it was the longest? And even longer with the appended "parable" about the brother, after which nothing else could be said? If one reads this parable as the first one, though, (without the one about the brother), then suddenly the question of the mother fits right there at its end, and Jesus answers her at once with the parable of the lost sheep . . .

After I discovered that, I found that the three parables of the "lost ones," if read in the order I have rearranged them here, produce an astounding theological tension. They give the answer to questions every person naturally has. Questions to which it seems God has not given an answer – but he does! We just need to switch the order of the three parables: in the beginning, the one of the lost son, then the one of the lost sheep and at the end the parable of the lost coin. Then answers come.

Let's turn first to the "lost son."

There is a family business. The father seems to be an experienced businessman; whatever he touches turns into a success. He has two sons; the older one is diligent, calm, and reliable, but without creativity and enthusiasm. The younger one instead has the makings of a playboy. He doesn't care about work, but more about parties and friends and leisure and luxuries. Having such a father allows him that sort of life; he's got everything. He lacks only one thing: he is not his own man. Without his father he would be helpless. Next to this father who knows and does everything better than he does, he will never rise. He will always be the nice, but superficial "sonny boy." As long as he throws parties, at least he is popular.

Then one day he becomes creative; he decides to step into the center himself and stand on his own two feet, with nobody above him. He wants to be someone big, like his dad. He asks to be paid his share of the estate, which at that time was a legitimate request. Now he is rich and can do whatever he wants. But the father knows his son; he knows that soon he is going to fall flat on his face because he has never learned to live responsibly, or to plan and give a certain order to his life. He doesn't have any self-discipline, doesn't know how to sacrifice, is immature. But the father knows, too, that the son will never find himself as long as he is in daddy's shadow. He needs to go off, needs to go through it himself, even if it will be bitter – only then will he have a chance to find himself.

Sometimes a little creative naiveté, which others might call stupidity, seems to lead life into a healthy direction.

(That holds true not only for teenagers going through adolescence, as nature has designed it, but also for many a faith-itinerary of young – or also older – people. One has to leave behind the "alter ego" of the Church, venturing into the foreign. Then we might find Jesus beyond the Church, find his countenance, and learn to recognize and love him; and through Jesus find the Church anew, carry it and bear with it).

The lad is now surrounded by crowds of friends; his golden credit card opens doors and hearts. He is extremely popular, enjoys the songs that are written for him, until one day the stream of money runs dry – and with it the friends disappear. He goes through something he had never experienced in himself. Sure, he could go back wailing and moaning to the good life in his father's house, but fortunately stubbornness and pride are awakening in him. "No," he says to himself, "I will not go crawling. The old man will not be proved right again. I will make it. I can do it!" But he has never learned to achieve anything, to fight against any sort of disinclination and laziness. He is slipping more and more. Hunger sets in. Maybe it would be easier abroad? He ends up with a job feeding a herd of swine, for the Jewish audience of the day the most horrible thing they could imagine. And then he sinks even deeper. Hunger drives him down among the swine: to have at least what they are feeding on in the mud . . .

Finally, he gives up. Not out of repentance or because he is coming to his senses, but for the simple reason that he is hungry. It is the natural urge for food that prepares the conversion. He recalls that the hired workers at his father's estate eat their good soup every day and he, the son, has nothing – only hunger. He experiences poverty. He has not even a crust of bread. This hunger instinct wins out over his pride, breaks his hollow ego. He gives up and plans his return.

What exactly motivated the son's conversion in the end, God alone knows. It is possible that at first his strategy is to be subservient. Traditionally, repentance and reason are hastily suggested as his only motive, but most attempts at interpretation do not take normal human nature into consideration. Whether the son planned his return out of insecurity, or embarrassment because his failure was so obvious, or out of calculation, or simply sheer fear, any of these are possible. Let's imagine he had written three phrases on his hand:

"Father, I have sinned against heaven and against you . . ." Oh that sounds good! Very submissive, father and heaven at the same level, yes, I am a sinner, full confession . . ." Next sentence: "I am not worthy any more to be your son . . ." Yes, yes, I did mess up, I realize that. You were always right, you are the best, I am worth nothing, I don't deserve anything. . . But now the third, and that's the point: "Let me be one of your hired hands . . ." Because they have food every day. And I am so hungry!

I chose a psychological approach for the interpretation of the parable. There are other approaches, such as in salvation history, in which the son who runs away from home represents the Gentiles and the other son, who is always with the father, represents the chosen people of God. Surely other models have also developed the parable in all its wisdom and beauty. The psychological approach has the advantage that many people in one way or another go through what I describe and reflect upon here. It can lead them to a more conscious understanding of their own life. From this understanding an order can develop for a better future.

In my interpretation, at the root of the son's "conversion" are therefore not repentance and reason, or even penance, but simply hunger! Nature with its instincts at times initiates conversion of soul and spirit. God uses everything – sometimes the weather, joyful circumstances or misfortune, terrible tragedies or catastrophes – to slowly, carefully, and gently turn us to himself.

Thus, the son turns around and sets out on his long way back. The way back with its difficulties becomes an inner conversion for him, both unexpectedly and unintendedly, and changes and renews him in the process of going home to the father. "But while he was still far off, his father saw him and was filled with compassion; he ran and put his arms around him and kissed him" (Lk 15:20).

God never loses sight of the human person – no one, ever. No matter how much a person may have strayed from God, God keeps an eye on them. He knows and senses and feels what is stirring in them. He has compassion on them! Not a word of wrath, of punishment or judgment, no "grumbling" or anger, no! Compassion instead! According to Jewish legalistic thinking, it would have been more fitting *not* to have any compassion on such a sinner. After all, he got himself into this mess all by himself. It's his own fault. He has sold himself to mammon – and one cannot have compassion with those who serve strange gods. Rather such a one should be stoned (see Dt 13:9-11).

But there was also the other theology: If one of my people cries out to me because he is treated unjustly, I will listen; for I am compassionate (see Ex 22:26) – and yet, the son had not been treated unjustly!

Every poor wretched person will know that God has compassion on him or her. Compassion is not just a word or a sentiment for Jesus, but it sets free in him the power to heal. In the parable, joy is set free through the father's compassion for his newly found son, joy that wants to celebrate. Celebrating can heal.

Jesus gives a practical description here of how judgment happens with him! There is no meticulous probing of guilt, no accusation, no demand for penance and submission, no punishment, no "throwing into *Gehenna*" – instead, the father runs towards the son. God runs towards the human person; he embraces and kisses each of us. That is his judgment: signs that are proof of his love, of forgiveness, of joy and self-giving union.

The son – Jesus has described this in a way that in psychological terms is extremely apt – seems to be completely dumbfounded, nearly numb, he *does not get* what is going on; something totally different should have been happening . . . Maybe he steals a furtive glance into the palm of his hand where the sentences are written. And then something marvelous happens: he cites the first sentence: "Father, I have sinned against heaven and against you . . ." and the second one: "I am not worthy anymore to be your son . . ." And the third sentence, the important one, with the goal to get food? It is missing! He does not say it anymore. The hunger is already satisfied through the embrace of the father, through receiving the newly experienced unity.

Just as with the Samaritan woman at the well in Sychar. She came to draw water, important for nature – but she runs away without her water jug! Her soul is filled with the life-giving eternal water. It is the same here for the son:

he no longer needs anything for the stomach, his hunger is satisfied. In the arms of the father everything is well.

Then the party begins: the best outfit, a ring on his finger, shoes on his feet, fetch the fattened calf, we want to eat, drink, and be merry! (Why are there so few images in our churches in which we can see the father and the son celebrating with sinners, laughing, and enjoying themselves because unity has been renewed?) The son has matured, he has found himself through his forlornness, through living in strange lands, through suffering poverty and through the difficult way back into the arms of the one who welcomes him with joy.

But – and now comes the great *BUT* of the woman in my retreat, her question: Yes Jesus, you said that well, I can feel for the father – but what if the son does *not* return? What if he cannot come back? If he is so stuck in the mud, in drugs and alcohol, so caught up in bad company that he cannot come back anymore? Does the father remain calmly, coolly sitting at home in his beautiful house, saying in the end: "It's his own fault, this good-for-nothing unfortunate son of mine!"?

What does God do if a person is no longer able to return? Is that person lost? Does God fold his hands and allow him to remain lost?

Jesus answered this question as though he had anticipated it. Yes, he knew that we would have to ask this. Because, it is said that God has given us freedom, and if with this freedom we decide against God, and follow our own ways, then that would be our own decision and God would respect it . . . But no EMT seeing a severely injured person on the highway will "respect" their "freedom" to drive recklessly, and leave the person lying there . . .

How much less the Originator of our faith, which derives from the heart of the Father! He thinks and acts altogether differently than we do. As an answer to such human thinking, Jesus formulated the parable of the lost sheep:

A person had a hundred sheep and one of them gets lost . . . We need to pause here already because that is not our environment anymore. None of us owns a hundred sheep. Maybe we have never even seen so many sheep, even from a distance. None of us has been wandering with them day and night out in the open. When I was in the Judaic desert, I encountered a young Bedouin who was tending his seventy sheep and goats, searching for grass among the stones and rocks, or in Beersheba a little girl, who early in the morning drove ten goats and sheep up the hills, I had a sense of hardly knowing this world at all. Therefore, we need to approach Jesus' parable slowly, in order not to interpret too much in the wrong way.

When the Bedouin drives his herd together at night, he realizes that one of the sheep is missing. This tells us that the shepherd has a personal relationship with his animals, can call each of them by name. Therefore, he notices if, among a hundred, one is missing. He knows them well and keeps an eye on them.

Countercheck: On Sundays do we priests notice if among a hundred parishioners one is missing? Do we ask about the one who is missing? Do we inquire about them until we find them, in the hospital, or having decided not to come back? Or having joined a different church?

Naturally, the shepherd also has dogs with him to keep such a big herd together and protect it. Nonetheless, one of the animals did escape. This little sheep had always had its little escapades: a little grass on the right, a little bush to the left of the path, then the beautifully smelling herbs behind the rock, in the valley some delicious-tasting flowers . . .

Not only did its escapades demand the special attention of the shepherd, but they also triggered anger and envy in the good sheep: "What nerve it has!" "That's outrageous!" "The shepherd needs to intervene!" "He can't let that pass!" "It's supposed to trot along just like the rest of us!"

Then, one day a pitiful "baa-baa" came from far away, hardly audible . . . "Finally!" "It had to happen!" "We knew it!" "That could not have ended well." "That was not supposed to go well." "God is just." "We got rid of this troublemaker." "Now peace and quiet has returned to our parish . . ."

And then the unfathomable happens. The shepherd orders his four dogs to circle the ninety-nine carefully – and he himself moves into the direction of the fearful cries of the lost sheep. He finds the one he is searching for, who – naturally out of curiosity – tripped too close to a deep cistern, narrow at the top and wide at the bottom, and slipped into its opening. Now it is lying on the bottom, on the swampy ground. It cannot save itself. It is lost. It can only cry for help.

Let's switch to the level of theology and faith. The parable, as we said in the beginning, wants to say something about God, about how God deals with sinners, with those who are lost. We can expect a crescendo in this parable, an increase above all in forlornness. This little sheep cannot return anymore, like the lost son could. It is truly lost. Strength, willpower, reason, or nature are too weak. Caught in its carelessness, in its disobedience, in life's circumstances – it does not matter in what – it will perish. Crying out is all it can do.

But now, with God, there is a crescendo.

When someone is so far lost, God does not remain sitting at home. No, he leaves his house and gets on his way. The ninety-nine obedient ones who truly would have "deserved" the care and attention of their shepherd need to be patient now, because the one who is lost needs him more than the others at this extremely precarious moment. It is an "imposition" on the obedient ones, but an imposition out of love, so that the herd may remain together without exception and loss. God freely gives his grace, first and foremost to those who need it more. That is why the Good Shepherd risks his own life, lowers himself on a rope into the pit to save the forlorn little sheep, lift it out of the mud and the swamp. He climbs down to where a person can no longer save themselves.

If a person cannot return, God returns to the person. To save the lost one. That is our image of God, our faith.

God does not throw anyone into *Gehenna*. On the contrary, he pulls them out.

Let's return to our group at the retreat. The woman is still sitting there. Now the tears pouring down her cheeks have turned into tears of joy. But then she lifts her head and asks once more: "But what if a person can't even cry for help anymore? If he or she is dead, inside and out, doesn't care anymore about God, about life? If a person does not want anything anymore, nothing, only to be obliterated, without any contact with anyone? What does God do then?"

Jesus answered this question too, with the answer of his Father in heaven, a treasure wrapped in the parable of the lost coins.

Had the evangelist Matthew, who prefers the number three, included this parable, he would have placed it in the middle of the "three lost ones," because Matthew most often places the main message at the center, to hold everything together. Maybe Luke adopted that idea here, too.

"What woman having ten silver coins, if she loses one of them. . ." (Lk 15: 8).

At the height of his revelation about how God is and works, Jesus depicts God in the form of a woman. Probably because a woman, a mother, searches longer than a man. The man gives up the search after five, seven, nine days, after no results, no prospect of finding anything. A woman never gives up searching. A mother's search does not abandon hope. Therefore, in this story, Jesus had to have a woman as the main character.

She has lost a coin. She lights a candle and sweeps the whole house . . .

A coin, a drachma, is a lifeless thing. The drachma cannot walk, it cannot call. It is an image of something dead, inside as well as out. And this dead thing even rolls away and disappears. It is the height of "being lost."

The Greek word Luke uses for "house" is *oikía,* a common word for "house," which was also used to mean a "room." The houses of poor people consisted of only one room with no windows, with the animals sleeping at the entrance at night. The floor of such a house was not made of wood or of tiles, but most probably was stamped-down soil. Often the dirt would be made from the rubble of previous houses that had stood on that site. Perhaps there was some kind of carpet in the middle of the room. If a coin would have rolled away in such a place, it could easily get stuck in a crack, in the old debris, among stones from previous houses. It would have become dirty and dull, and it would have been nearly impossible to find. So, the woman takes a broom, lights a lamp, and searches . . .

She searches "carefully, until she finds it."

That is the secret of the heart of God, a God full of love. For God, nothing is lost or undetectable. God searches until he finds.

The Greek word that our translation describes as "carefully" can also mean "having at heart." This resonates because God has every "lost" person at heart and he searches not only one day, not only ten days, not only for an eternity. He searches until . . . *until* he finds! He will not begin his heavenly banquet for all peoples until he has carried the last lost person home on his shoulders and put that one at the reserved place in the celebration.

The measure of our being lost, for God, becomes the measure of his search. The more *inactive* a person, the more *active* God will become, until he finds the one who is lost.

The murderer on the cross who asks for help is like the sheep calling out for help. The thief on the other side, who does not even beg for help anymore, is like the lost coin and in his case, God's love becomes boundless, until he finds him too.

At the end, as with the lost sheep, there is a celebration in heaven and earth: God wants to celebrate with all those who have been found again. That means all of us, each one. God calls everyone together, from the right and the left, to celebrate with him. Where is the image of this God rejoicing, yes, boundlessly rejoicing, because he has found those who were lost?

Of course, God rejoices also over those who don't have to convert, as the Gospel says, but he rejoices more, much more, over even one sinner who returns, who converts and becomes a new creation in the arms of the motherly Father who comes running towards him.

Most probably, the disciples were present at this conflict with the Pharisees and scribes. Was Judas there, too? Did he perhaps sit at the table with tax collectors and sinners and eat with them too? Did he perhaps hear the parable of the lost coin? A day will come for him when he will hold such a silver piece in his hands – actually, thirty of them – and he will throw them away, so that they roll off and are lost. No one will go looking for them.

Will he remember on that day the one coin that rolled away and was lost? But which the Master himself searched for, on his knees, three times on his bleeding knees, until he found it?

With this coin, did Jesus describe the end of his friend, Judas? Not only his end on earth, but his fulfillment in heaven?

And something else is hidden in this parable of the lost coin:

According to the custom of the Bedouins, which still holds true today, a man loses his honor if his wife loses something that belongs to him. In this story, she lost a coin, and therefore, the man lost his honor, because the woman was unreliable. Jesus has chosen this cultural circumstance to depict the Son of God's boundless search (in the image of a woman), by clothing himself in the person of the woman and searching until the coin was found. He wants to say that he is not unreliable before his Father in Heaven. He will search until – figuratively speaking – the Father's honor will be restored. He will find what belongs to the Father. He will prove himself reliable.

It is to satisfy his Father's honor that Jesus finds and recovers all sinners, all people, and celebrates a feast with them.

Excursion
Putting our life in order

A fourth objection could, and should, be raised to what I said in the previous chapter. If it is true that God is boundless in his search for all sinners, and that he will search until he finds, and if it is true that the pitiful state of a person becomes God's measure for an even greater search, can we human beings not just go ahead and sin, shrug our shoulders and live according to our own desires? Won't God take the initiative and save us anyhow?

Already in the times of St. Paul, Christians in Rome came up with that idea, and Paul had to answer clearly: "What then are we to say? Should we continue in sin in order that grace may abound? By no means! "(Rm 6:1-2).

Surely this remains: "Where sin increased, grace abounded all the more "(Rm: 5:20). That is the fundamental truth. That is the way God acts.

But how does the human person act?

Those who live according to their own wishes and desires have not yet reached the level of love, of a relationship in which you give of yourself, just as God has done with us, and in which we shall grow into him, so that this may become the guiding principle of humanity. In this personal relationship of love, once we recognize and have experienced it, a human person *cannot* continue to lean back with an attitude of laziness and self-centeredness, and let God do everything. On the contrary, he or she will offer themselves to God at *his* service and "wear themselves out" for the kingdom of God – not out of fear or obligation, but out of gratitude and joy. The person responds out of a deeply perceived love that cannot but answer lovingly to the love of God. Love does not count the cost.

Even when I was a child in postwar Berlin, we experienced this. Of course, our parents took care of us and looked after us always and without conditions. It was their selfless care for us that awakened in us children a sense of gratitude, and with it the readiness to give our contribution to our family life. In the face of our parents' loving care, we could no longer be lazy and let our parents do everything.

A second factor: God wants to save, and God will save everyone. But if after a self-centered, destructive life devoid of love, someone will be transformed "as through fire" in purgatory, God also wants to protect that person from great suffering. No one will be excused from the "heavenly rehab." Therefore, our time here on earth is about putting our life in order according to the standard of love, of serving one another. Only through this kind of giving for one another will a person find happiness. Only in this way will all people live together in peace, going beyond every border, and all differences, which, stimulating and enriching, are going to remain.

But how do we bring order into our life that will foster happiness, so that at the end we can look back at a fulfilled and meaningful life – and confidently look towards the transformation which God will give us? An anecdote: In the mid 90's, I was bringing aid to Estonia as part of my assistance project. I was using a truck and took it on a freight ferry across the Baltic Sea. Occasionally one might be the only passenger on such a ferry and can walk around everywhere. On that day it was very, very foggy and I climbed up to the captain's bridge, wanting to watch how the captain was steering the old barge through that gray wall of fog. I could not even see the prow of the ship. And then I discovered something which I believe is of utmost importance.

The captain had his radar switched on. He flipped the first switch, and I could see a few white dots on the screen, which was set at twenty-five nautical miles. Every point indicated another ship, he explained to me, and showed me our dot. Then he flipped a second switch and lines were added to the dots. With that, I learned, one could see the direction in which every single ship was moving. A third switch: numbers were added to the lines, they showed the course of any given ship – and with great concern I saw that some of the lines were crossing. But the view in the fog outside didn't show anything! A fourth switch and the radar calculated which ships would collide if they kept their course, and in how many minutes that collision would occur . . .

But through the fog, one did not see the danger.

This is a parable for every person's life. Throughout our whole life, day in and day out, each one of us is guided by our soul and by whatever takes place within it. Innumerable factors guide and determine our behavior, our actions, our speaking, and our reactions. For some people, one could predict that if they continue living like that, there will be a crash. I can see a catastrophe coming. If you are not going to change your life, you are going to sink. The bad thing here is that the untrained person who does not have "radar eyes," does not see the danger and continues to plow through the fog of their life. Once they see the danger, it is usually already too late.

The Samaritan woman at the well in Sychar probably had an idea that through her behavior she would continue to run into collisions and would eventually sink among tears and people's whispered gossip. However, she didn't know how she could avoid the catastrophe. Just as the younger son in Jesus' parable could have foreseen where and how his life was going to end if he did not seek counsel or find a good "helmsman" who was able to guide him.

And Judas? He might not have thought enough about the course his life was taking – and about the course Jesus' life was taking. He didn't pay attention to what, in hidden ways, was guiding him, steering him in a direction that eventually had to lead to a collision. He did not allow any "captain" to indicate to him a critical direction that he could have followed. It was not much different for the other apostles.

Every person needs to have a clear picture of the course of his or her life. For that, one needs orientation marks and experience, and something or someone who makes what is still invisible visible.

In earlier times, when people would sail across the oceans, there were some who knew how to determine the ship's course and direction by the stars at night and by the sun by day; others looked for, and hired, experienced "sea dogs" who, with their knowledge, experience, and common sense, would find the right way. Today pilots come on board a ship once it enters the harbor. Similarly, without air traffic controllers, no plane could safely land. Or think of our insurance policies – they compel us to have preventive care. If you continue to drink or smoke, if you don't have this or that tested, and, if needed, be treated, you could face a serious illness, and "we won't pay for that." For the same reason, of course, our cars need frequent inspections . . .

We give attention to our bodies and our cars . . .

And what about our souls?

Once I had to go to the emergency room at a big hospital. The doctor soon determined that there was nothing seriously wrong with me. We started talking. She asked me: "What is your profession?" I told her I did pastoral care for priests. She was interested and wanted to know what that was and how it works. When I explained it to her, she said spontaneously: "You might as well start right here with us medical doctors . . ."

Today big companies hire so-called "compliance officers." Scandals, bribery, manipulation of every kind and excessive waste that has been uncovered nearly everywhere in the past years have led to a call for such compliance officers. Their task is to ensure discipline and order, manage legal and regulatory issues, as well as adherence to ethical standards and requirements. In other words, they are something like a confessor for the company, but are not bound to secrecy. On the contrary, they need to intervene – if they do not get outmaneuvered by one of the chief officers in the process!

In the Catholic Church in Germany, the sacrament of reconciliation, confession, is in decline. In some places it has already disappeared, whereas the Lutheran Church is taking timid steps towards confession finding a home in its parishes. In many places, clergy have prepared beautiful reconciliation services during Lent. Yet, in some parishes, the "confessional," that time-honored, proven spot for giving order and guidance to one's life, has become a storage room for old chairs. In the United States the sacrament of confession has been in decline since the mid 60's but has remained a staple for many of the faithful.

Perhaps God is telling us that for today's times, a new "radar" is needed, a new means to navigate safely through the fog of your life.

People continue searching for someone with whom they can speak to bring some order to their lives and find meaning and goals for their daily activities. The few priests we still have often do not have the time for such conversations or they have too little training. Such talks, should they be helpful, can take a long time and might happen during a walk, and not in the confessional. Thus, people go anywhere where someone will listen to them. Our Church's traditional offer of confession is hardly in demand in the same way it was in the past.

But the distress is there. Everywhere the same distress.

More than twenty years ago, Jesuits rediscovered the institution of "spiritual accompaniment." Such spiritual companions have been around since the first centuries of Christendom, among the first monks in the Egyptian desert or in Asia Minor with Basil the Great or Benedict, the father of Western Monasticism. The *starets*, too, who were the elders of Eastern Orthodox monasteries, are counted among the "helping companions"; the monks on Mount Athos were for a long time the center of the *starets* tradition.

With the sacramentalization of the life of the Church, the institution of the "spiritual companion" took a back seat, whereas today, it seems, God himself is calling it to the forefront again.

These spiritual companions don't need to be ordained by the Church. They can be men or women, and do not necessarily need to have completed any studies. They can be young or old – but they need to have experience, live by the Scriptures, and be at home with Christ. They must be meek, trustful, discreet, and loving. Often, they have gone through dark nights in their own life, and out of this experience of being powerless, they have become meek and wise. They do not give long lectures. They listen, sense the distress of the other person, relate to what makes him or her suffer, and give advice, sometimes with just a few words. But they address the issue.

The spiritual companion steps back from him or herself and lets God's Spirit work.

We do have these spiritual companions. But they are too few. Of course, it is advisable that they have sufficient education. Once they become aware of their responsibility, they usually become aware of that need, and study practical psychology in order to connect written knowledge with their own experience and thus be better able to help. (There are also opportunities to be trained as a spiritual companion.)[10] They need to understand when a "particular case" goes beyond their capabilities and a specialist needs to be involved.

However, it is mostly about very normal, basic questions. What am I influenced by? What aggravates me? When do I feel restless? What makes me unhappy? What fears do I have? How do others see me?

Generally, it is enough to meet with such a companion every six months, but sometimes more frequent encounters are advisable, and this can go on for a long time. In these conversations, it is most important to define and formulate a goal to move toward in my life. What should my life be about, first and foremost? What would give me a deep peace? What would allow me to look back at something meaningful at the end of my life?

Even someone who turned out to be a maniac or a dictator was once a "normal" child and a normal teenager. How much might have been prevented, or guided onto the right path, if someone with kindness and a watchful eye had accompanied such persons! But not everything can be prevented. Jesus could not prevent (or did he allow it with open eyes?) that two of his twelve disciples became traitors or denied him, even though they had been with him every day.

A spiritual companion is not immune to situations of helplessness. Nonetheless, he or she won't interfere in a controlling way, in no way will decide for the other person, or manipulate them, and "create a creature of his or her own." In faith he or she will count on God, who is in charge and

---

10. Catholic colleges often offer these courses. In some locations you can be certified by the local diocese.

even beyond death guides everything towards good. But he or she will inquire and be attentive when in descriptions something is omitted, something is passed over, when unfiltered emotions push reason aside, or when the eyes or speech betray that the person is avoiding some insight. That takes a lot of patience. Pope Francis speaks of this as the "martyrdom of patience."

Underneath all of this lies the wisdom that, before all else, it is our soul, with its innumerable impulses, that "drives" us, dominates us, creates our "mood," from which good and bad develop. None of these impulses are good or bad in themselves. On the contrary, they are all good, created by the Creator to work towards what is good – but every impulse, if not tamed and pruned, can lead to evil, destructive consequences.

In fact, the modulation of the voice can give an insight into the mood of the person. The greatest part of who we are develops not so much in our mind, but in the many layers of our soul. Those, in turn, are subject to countless influences, often from early childhood, influences of which we might not even be consciously aware. The experienced spiritual companion recognizes these influences; he or she can be compared to an "early-warning system" that senses the variations of the invisible ocean floor from which tsunamis can later arise.

Everything we briefly mentioned here about the individual person can also be applied to big companies. Also, and most of all, to the management floors in corporations, sports organizations, banks, churches . . . . Experience tells us that the higher up the ladder someone is, the more difficult they might find it to let themselves be accompanied. Yet, those who are leading others should be especially concerned with themselves and have a spiritual companion by their side – not just a nutritionist and exercise coach. But experience shows that it is those who are going through life pretty well who tend to look for a spiritual companion, while those who really would need it (and everyone around them can see it) strictly decline every accompaniment, declaring it absolutely unnecessary.

We need to be prepared for a Church with fewer and fewer priests. For confession though, a priest is necessary. Confession provides sacramental forgiveness of sins. But after my experience over forty-five years of hearing confessions, I can say that confessed sins are mostly about the individual's problems in daily life, which one cannot deal with on their own. Confession and forgiveness of sins then may be an "initial" means for a person to become aware of their problems. However, in the long run it is not enough if we want to help that person adequately. It needs the complement of long-term conversations and exchange. "What helps me the most to find what I am looking for?" is a fundamentally helpful question. Today more and more people have trouble relating to the concept of "sin," which is logical because "sin" is most of all about a personal relationship with Jesus Christ. If this has become meaningless for me or is missing altogether, "sin" and "confession" remain only empty words. Spiritual accompaniment is a service which, through conversations and reflection, can prepare the way to a vivid, renewed relationship with Christ, and alert our conscience to what we call "sin."

A radar for one's everyday life

What if there is not a good spiritual companion where I am? What if I need to drive a great distance, and this good person has time to see me only rarely? Is there another solution, a radar that can safely navigate me through the fog of my everyday life, through my routine?

Yes, there is such a "radar." But at the outset I need to know in what direction I want to head. What is my goal? It is extremely necessary to spend time thinking about my goal in life, every year reviewing anew what matters most of all to me. It will be reflected in all I do. How do I want to be known? When Basil the Great called his communities of friars into being in Pontus (today's southeastern Turkey) he wrote a rule for them that consisted of phrases from the Gospels. It is a simple method to which anyone can apply themselves. I read the Gospels and write down the phrases of Jesus that speak to me, and seem fitting to shape my life, and beneficial for the goal I seek. Such phrases might be: "give to my brother or sister at the right time what they need for their life," or "what I want to have done to me, do onto others," or "be merciful as your heavenly Father is merciful," or "love one another."

If you read through the Gospel you will be surprised how many such principles for a successful, meaningful life you find in Jesus' words and actions. With time, and each person should take that time, you can sense the phrase that most appeals to you: which sentence do *I* want to live and conform my will and actions to? Which phrase do I want to put into practice? One phrase is enough. But that one sentence needs to be taken to heart anew every day. I can write it down and keep it close to me, or in my pocket, so that it always reminds me.

A captain who doesn't know which harbor he is heading to doesn't need radar. If someone leaves the house without having a goal, it is meaningless and indifferent whether he makes a right or a left turn. Meaning and direction is always dictated by the goal. Those who do not have a goal in life don't know whether they are living in the right or the wrong way. Such individuals cannot correct themselves, and ultimately feel uneasy. Setting a goal for oneself, living for a goal and structuring one's days by it, is a fundamental human ability and need. In every field of business, sports, or the military, one first brings into focus a goal, and then asks how best to get there. All too often this is forgotten in considering the most important aspect of life, that is, the soul. It is necessary to ask of myself: What will be the goal of my life?

Once I find and formulate such a goal for myself, I can build my day according to it. I would like to propose a simple method for this. It needs to be simple without requiring too much time, otherwise it might end up becoming a very short-lived practice. It is centered most of all on getting a sense of what controls and guides me under the surface.

Three key moments during the day keep me on course.

First: getting up in the morning. While I am still lying in bed or getting up, whether moaning or with legs swinging, I can simply say: "Lord, here I am again. I intend to go through the day with you. Today I will look for you, and search for you in everything" – if this is the goal that I have taken for myself. In the shower or getting ready, I surely have half a minute to look at the day and what it might bring. This is enough to prepare myself within and find God in everything. While I am getting dressed, I can mumble that I ultimately want to put on You, Jesus Christ, my Lord.

This practice should be so short and so simple that I never skip it. It is inserted in what I do anyhow every day, and therefore does not require any extra time. If I forget it, it's not a big deal, I will remember it tomorrow. The length of this practice is unimportant, what is important is the faithfulness to do it every day.

Second: lunchtime. We all have a different lunchtime routine. But everyone takes a moment in the middle of the day. What counts is to find a practice I can insert into something I am doing anyway, without taking extra time.

Like our cell phone, which nowadays always has priority. We say "sorry," if someone else is in the room, and answer a call. "Oh love, it's nice to hear your voice, how are things going?" . . . Silence . . . "I am happy too, yes, a couple of questions, problems, but we'll get through that . . . I am grateful you are there and look after me and us . . ." This is not the conversation of a wife with her husband, but the interior conversation of a person with their Maker, their "Beloved".

Or the following practice. We all go to the bathroom at lunchtime. Most probably there, at least there, we will be alone. Undisturbed. One can use that time, while washing our hands, to say: "Lord, cleanse all my thoughts, my desires, my impulses, take away all restlessness and aggression, make me become peaceful again, willing to listen and to talk, that I may spread the fragrance of your kindness . . ."

One has to have some imagination. That happens only if I really want it, seeing the reason and the necessity for such a practice. The practice of "saying grace" should always be part of every meal. At lunchtime we go to eat, whether in the cafeteria, on the street, in a restaurant, alone or at home with the children . . . we should always pause for a moment and pray, to thank God for having food, for being healthy, thinking of those who are hungry in that moment. Prayer should begin with the sign of the cross – others may, and should, see that I have a relationship with God, the Creator of heaven and earth. And even a non-believing medical doctor would agree that it is meaningful for soul, body, and spirit to pause for even half a minute of rest before starting to eat.

Third: evening. This practice might well be the most important. The end of the day looks different from one person to another, and the level of tiredness varies. But this is about winding down when everything is done, when even the TV does not distract me anymore and I can look back at the day, and ask myself: "What happened today? How did it go? How did I do overall?" One thing holds true also for this practice, maybe more than for the others: it should not cost us any effort, I should not be moaning at the thought already. Especially this practice at night should be easy, simple, inviting, relaxing. You should look forward to it. You can do it alone or together as a couple. Choose a comfortable armchair or sofa; a glass of wine can be helpful or a cup of tea or a beer – whichever way is good and perceived as restful. Relaxing and starting to unwind should be the outward atmosphere.

The inner structure of this practice at night has three phases:

(1) Start by recalling some of the fundamental revelations of our faith: that God was present in everything, he accompanied everything. He knows all the suffering of those I have encountered today and carries it together with them. He gives salvation. We are all moving towards him and his glory. He holds a place for everyone. He will fulfill and lead towards good what we cannot achieve here. He is, was, and will be in everything and above everything . . . All of this should be just a simple remembering, so that I can put myself into the space that is above everything, as the sky is above the earth, and the sky begins already at the tips of the grass.

(2) The next part consists in looking back at the day and considering what happened within ourselves, under the

surface. I call it the *reflectio* at night. I am presenting different ways to do this, so that the practice does not peter out or become a boring routine. An honest look at the day in retrospect, helped by one of these proposed ways, is in no way intended to blame or judge or criticize myself or look for sins. These are simply ways to take a good honest look, noticing the different moods and mood swings that guided me today. That is enough. Use only one way each evening, whichever is most appealing.

A: What feelings, moods, desires, sense of resistance have welled up in me since this morning? Which ones took the upper hand and dominated me for a longer time? How did I deal with them, or instead did they have a grip on me?

B: How did I feel physically today? Where did I feel discomfort? What did I perceive as a weight on my stomach, my liver, my heart? Did I get enough exercise? Did I hydrate sufficiently?

C: Which people, colleagues or co-workers, did I have closer contacts with today? Who did I try to be in contact with? Whom did I avoid? With whom has there been tension? Was the tension partly caused by me?

D: How do I look at my family, my workplace, my community? What kind of a group are we? What is my contribution to this group? Am I actively engaged, or more passive and trailing along? Or impeding and blocking?

E: Where, in which places, was I today? Whom did I encounter? What did I miss? Would I like to bless some of these people tonight? Look at them with kindness?

F: Were there small, brief moments today in which I experienced something like consolation or surprising joy?

G: What am I thankful for in a special way today? What gave me particular joy? Was I able to be the cause of joy for someone else? Have I overlooked moments of joy or didn't even notice them? Who wanted to give me joy today?

(3) The third phase of this prayer consists in giving thanks. Giving thanks means that I call to mind that everything today has been a gift; that everything could have turned out differently. It could be that I have been enriched, without noticing it.

Only the one who gives thanks lives in a conscious way and is prepared for times when something will not be there in the future, when times get tough and we might have to cut back. By giving thanks I build up stock in my faith and take on an attitude of being poor in spirit. By giving thanks my reserves are opened.

Giving thanks is the continuation of the Eucharist, the Church's great liturgical prayer of thanksgiving. To thank the Father with joy is the goal and fulfillment of our life, until we see God.

The thoughts presented here have been tried and practiced, yet they are only some of many possibilities that could be used. They should be a help for every person to give a meaningful order to life, and this brings happiness. One can practice these points alone or with others. For the latter though, it takes sensitivity and delicacy.

Everyone we have met in these pages, whether real persons or characters in Jesus' parables, could have used such "order" for their lives, or did, in fact, have it – Jesus surely did. Judas, to whom we want to pay closer attention, seemingly did not have this order or did not use it; and Peter used it too little. Even if his created beings go through life without this order, God saves them. Because *his* order ultimately orders our chaos, too.

God gives his salvation

This chapter will take a parallel look at two people who in their time were considered sinners. They encountered Jesus, or better, he encountered them. Jesus approached *them*. The initiative was his. Let's see how he "carried these people home," and get a sense whether they could create an order for their life from it.

It cannot be ruled out that Judas was present at both encounters. What effect could Jesus' behavior have had on him? Was he drawn to the salvation given to people, or did he reject it?

One encounter took place in a noble villa, the other in a regular synagogue. In one, Jesus encountered a rich person, in the other, someone very poor. In one, it was a man, in the other, a woman; one was far from the faith of Israel, the other searching for faith; one was healthy, the other very sick; but both heard the same word: "son of Abraham, daughter of Abraham," and to both, salvation was given, the new *home* of God.

One is the wealthy chief tax collector, Zacchaeus (Lk 19:1-10), the other is an unnamed crippled woman (Lk 13:10-17). Probably too seldom are these two encounters between Jesus and sinners compared to see where they match and how they differ. If we venture to do this, the characteristics of each come out in an even more impressive and beautiful way.

The tax collector, Zacchaeus, is described by Luke as being very rich. He had accumulated a fortune, but he was also short in stature. The woman was short too, because she was bent over and crippled, but all she owned were a few pennies. Undoubtedly, her bent-over body had isolated her from other people. She was regarded as someone punished by God for some kind of sin, as was anyone who had an illness. Zacchaeus' short stature might lead us to conclude that he, too, was in some way isolated. People did not want to be friends with such a midget – unless they depended on him or could profit from him.

Both therefore were isolated, alone. But the woman knew that she was a sinner, or rather, should regard herself as one. Zacchaeus couldn't care less; he had lost God and heaven already. The woman wanted to hear Jesus in the synagogue; the chief tax collector was curious to see what such a prophet looked like. She went to the entrance of the synagogue; he climbed a tree.

We can imagine that the woman might have leaned on a column at the entrance – she did not dare enter. And being bent-over she could see Jesus only with difficulty – or not at all. She could only hear his voice.

Strangely enough it was not all that different for Zacchaeus. He wouldn't dare to be in the midst of the pious Jews (much less in a synagogue); they would have beaten him up, or worse. Thus, he remained behind the protecting wall of his property. He was not crippled, but he was short, and so he, too, had to come up with something to see Jesus. Zacchaeus climbed a tree for the sole purpose of seeing the extraordinary prophet. Both had a limited view, the woman because she was so bent-over, Zacchaeus because of the branches and leaves of the tree he was sitting in.

But both wanted to see Jesus, urged on by the curiosity of nature or, unbeknownst to them, of the soul.

And then they both hear the call. Zacchaeus hears his name; perhaps Jesus called him a couple of times, each time louder. The woman, whose name no one knows, is simply called forward and hears the word, "Woman." By calling these two people, the alleged sinner, Zacchaeus, and the old woman, allegedly punished by God, Jesus exposes himself to the rejection of "the people." The leader of the synagogue is appalled that the woman lets herself be healed on the Sabbath; the crowd in Jericho grumbles that Jesus intends to stay at the house of a sinner, who doesn't deserve that at all.

By staying with Zacchaeus, Jesus deliberately went against the purification laws of His religion. At the trial against Jesus, shortly after this visit to Zacchaeus' house, we hear that Caiaphas and the high priests could not enter the court building of Pilate, a Gentile, because it would make them "unclean" and, therefore, unable to eat the Paschal lamb (Jn 18:28). Jesus, however, goes into the house of the sinner, Zacchaeus. Of course, it is not because he wants to become "unclean," but rather so that salvation might also reach the one whose behavior has placed him far from the faith, who feels excluded by God. This because Jesus is the Paschal lamb given by God for the whole world. He goes everywhere. And wherever he goes, everything becomes pure.

In the synagogue, Jesus breaks another obvious command of the Torah: healing was not allowed on a Sabbath since the religious leaders had classified it as "work." But God had ordained the Sabbath in remembrance of the liberation of his people from Egypt (Dt 5:15) – and liberation from captivity is work, a highly complex activity! Here Jesus liberates a woman from the hands of "Satan"! Actually, he acts correctly according to ancient Jewish tradition.

In the eyes of the religious upper class of his time, Jesus was a "man of scandal." Jesus did not court the favor of the people or those in high office, but wanted to reveal God, his Father, as he is in truth. To do that he trespassed against commands and broke laws drawn up by religious leaders. By doing so, he risked his life, but he was willing to do even that if, in that way, he could rescue even just one sinner and grant that person salvation.

Looking in this way at Jesus and his dealing with those regarded as sinners, one would tend to think that he was not interested in their respective sins. Neither with the Samaritan woman, nor in the parable of the three lost ones, nor with Zacchaeus, and even less with this woman, since she had not broken any commandment. No, in fact, for Jesus, sin is not at the center, but the salvation he wants to give. He does not look for sin in a person's life, but for love.

Will it be different with Judas?

For the moment, let us return to the synagogue filled with men: Just imagine how the woman, called by Jesus, now walks through the midst of them, finding her way, shaking and quivering, bent over . . . how would it be today if an open-minded Imam called a woman to come forward through the midst of the men . . . knowing that according to people's understanding she is not allowed to do that?

With Zacchaeus, something even stronger happens because Jesus says to this *mega-sinner*: "Today I must stay at your house!" Doesn't that evoke the image of Abraham who hosted the three men who came to be his guests (Gen 18)? Zacchaeus' efforts are a generous attempt to restore any injustice he had done, in order to "deserve" this guest, but Jesus doesn't mention sin and repentance – just as the merciful father neither lists his son's offences nor even wants to hear them. He does not ask for penance – because God wants to give freely, at no cost, without conditions. God does not demand anything but rejoices over what this person understood: "Today salvation has come to this house!"

What reason does Jesus offer for giving such a gift? This is breathtaking, with Zacchaeus as well as with the crippled woman. Jesus calls each of them, "Son of Abraham," "Daughter of Abraham." One must know that for the Jews, Abraham was the father of humanity; from him stemmed all nations. Therefore, in our language, "Son or daughter of Abraham" means, "because that person is a human being!" That is sufficient for the true God.

One does not need to belong to a certain religion or to a certain church or community or be a "believer" or even a saint – it is sufficient to be a human being. Always, also as a sinner, one is a created being of God, the motherly Father of all, who turns towards everyone.

This is wonderful. This is our faith.

Jesus explains one more time for Zacchaeus how he will hold judgment: "For the Son of Man has come to seek out and to save the lost." Judgment therefore is not an instrument of condemnation, punishment, or rejection, but setting things straight again, straightening out everything through the loving attention given by God. Every human being's life is made *right*, redeemed through God's "setting things straight again." In the three parables of the "lost ones," Jesus depicted that concept in images; here he does so with real people.

What follows – and how could it be otherwise! – is a festive meal. A celebration! That's what the good father and the shepherd and the woman do, too, when they find again what they had lost (also the Samaritan woman with the people in the village). Now Zacchaeus, the one "far from God" (who is not far anymore because God took up his dwelling with him!) celebrates a great feast. Just as Jacob said in his time: "Surely the Lord is in this place – and I did not know it! . . . This is none other than the house of God, and this is the gate of heaven" (Gen 28:16-17). Zacchaeus too, will say this later, when he thinks back on that day.[11]

---

11. Tradition says that Zacchaeus – a little man with a big bishop's miter – became the first bishop of Caesarea Maritima and there, we assume, Luke met him while he waited for Paul to be released from prison (between 59 and 61).

But what about the feast of the woman who is not bent over anymore, who stands there upright and looks Jesus in the eye? For her we do not hear of a festive meal, only that "the entire crowd was rejoicing." Was there no feast? Or does not the joy of the people already indicate the beginning of a feast? Can't we take this feast for granted, after everything we have heard and lived with them? Her celebration would have been in great poverty and simplicity. It would have looked very different from the feast with Zacchaeus, because the woman was in no position to give a feast, was in no way prepared. Yes, she was in no position to do so. When last had she given a party? She had gone to the synagogue as a crippled woman – and now? Of course, she wanted to celebrate, invite this prophet – but, oh, how embarrassing that would be! Her shack . . . Zacchaeus had a beautiful villa, many slaves, rich golden housewares . . . She had nothing. A couple of square feet of floor, a stool, a cup and a plate made of clay, maybe with a broken rim . . . how could she celebrate?

Yet I am sure she wanted to!

Sure, Luke mentioned the feast of the poor only remotely, but for me it is hard to imagine that Jesus did *not* go with the woman. Alone, of course. And surely, he filled her poor shack with the splendor of heaven. Like with the Samaritan woman, both would have enjoyed the tea, both from the same cup, as though it were made of gold, and as though the wine were from Cana, and the two of them must have laughed – with the woman looking at him . . . looking at him without end.

Visio beatifica.

As we will do on our great feast at the end of our days.

Judas, the friend

Jesus called his apostle Judas, the one who delivered him to the high priests, "friend": "Friend, do what you are here to do" (Mt 26:50). In the Old Testament, Abraham, too, is called "the friend of God." Can we conclude anything from this parallel?

Abraham is mentioned twice as "friend of God," once by God in Isaiah 41:8: "But you . . . Jacob, whom I have chosen, the offspring of Abraham, my friend "(*Khalil Abraham*), and also in 2 Chronicles 20:7: "Did you not, O our God, drive out the inhabitants of this land before your people Israel, and give it for ever to the descendants of your friend Abraham?" In the New Testament, it is James who reminds us of this honorary title: "'Abraham believed God, and it was reckoned to him as righteousness,' and he was called the friend of God" (Jas 2:23). A "friend of God," therefore, is one who trusts in God, even if the reality does not seem to support this trust. In Genesis 15:6 (the text James refers to), we do not find the word "friend," but we can assume it to be deeply rooted in Jewish tradition.

Is Judas Iscariot a friend of God, too? Did he trust his Master?

In Greek, the noun for "friend" is "*philos.*" Thus, Jesus is called by the crowd the "friend [*philos*] of tax collectors and sinners" (Mt 11:19). Luke is the one who uses this word most frequently since he writes for the Romans. Four times he calls the man who comes to visit at night asking for bread "friend" (Lk 11:5-8). When thousands of people stream in to hear Jesus, he calls them "my friends" (Lk 12:4). One may well say that Luke maintains an indiscriminate, unproblematic use of the word "friend." Mark does not use the term at all. John mentions Jesus' words: "Our friend Lazarus has fallen asleep" (Jn 11:11). And Jesus tells the apostles (Judas is no longer with them at that moment, but isn't he included?): "I have called you friends" (Jn 15:13-15).

The quality of the word *philos* becomes clear by the fact that it can be used for *love*. Here are just a few quotations: "Jesus, he whom you love [*phileís*], is ill" (Jn 11:3), referring to Lazarus. In the following conversation with his friend, Simon Peter, who denied him, Peter says three times: "Yes, Lord, you know that I love [*philô*] you" (Jn 21:15-17). John mentions another word for "love" *agapáō*, but we will not look into this here (this term was used to express Jesus' love for Martha, Mary and Lazarus, see Jn 11:5).

One could also use a second word for "friend": *hetaîros*. Matthew is the only one who uses it twice in Jesus' parables. Once he uses it in the parable of the workers in the vineyard. The "landowner" addresses the angry spokesman with it: "Friend, I am doing you no wrong" (Mt 20:13). Then Jesus' parable ends with a fundamental manifestation of the landowner's (God's) intention, whose self-giving love has no boundaries: "I will give the last one just as much as I give to you!" Once again, *the last will be first.*

In the parable of the man who comes without festive clothes to the wedding, he, too, is addressed by the king as "friend" [*hetaîre*] (Mt 22:12).

With the same word Jesus addresses his apostle, Judas, when he is arrested in the garden of Gethsemane: *hetaîre* (Mt 26:50). Its meaning is closer to "companion, comrade, pal," but also "friend." Therefore, *hetaîre* indicates that the quality of the relationship is a little below that of being a friend.

Being aware of the subtle differences, maybe we can put them aside now and follow the common translation, according to which in Gethsemane, as he is being taken captive,

Jesus says to Judas: "Friend [*hetaĩre*], do what you are here to do"(Mt 26:50). By his choice of words, Jesus expressed that Judas is lacking the trust that distinguished Abraham.

Was Judas perhaps on the way to reach this full trust and friendship?

To trace the person of Judas Iscariot is pretty difficult because indications in the Gospels about him are scarce, widely divergent, and mixed with interpretations and personal prejudice. Furthermore, for over 2000 years the tradition of the Church has branded him as the culprit of Jesus' death: He denounced Jesus! If he had not done that, Jesus would not have had to die . . .

Is that really so? How did Judas, as far as we know, get this negative image? Because he sold his master for thirty lousy pieces of silver?

Let us take a closer look. According to Mark (14:10-11), Judas offers the high priests to hand Jesus over to them – and only thereafter they, out of their own initiative, promise to give him money in return. In Matthew, however, Judas first asks how much money they will give him if he hands Jesus over to them.

The amount, "thirty pieces of silver," recounted only by Matthew, is mentioned in the book of Exodus (21:32), as the price for a slave who has been gored and killed by a bull, payable by the bull's owner. In this context, then, by paying that amount the high priests would scornfully be saying that Jesus was not worth more than a dead slave.

In Zechariah (11:12-13), we read once more about thirty pieces of silver. This text states that certain people wanted to get rid of a "good shepherd" sent by God, for thirty shekels of silver – in this case, the disgrace would not lie with Judas, but with "certain people."

But Matthew links this scene to another event in the Scriptures, passed on to us by Jeremiah (18:1-17). For thirty pieces of silver the high priests, as Matthew recounts, have bought the potter's field as a burial place for strangers (Mt 27:6-10). Jeremiah had taken the work of a potter as an image, a potter who continuously starts over when the object in his hands does not turn out well. It is an image of God regretting the good that he promised his people: "Look, I am a potter shaping evil against you. . . Turn now, all of you from your evil way. . . But my people have forgotten me, they burn offerings to a delusion. . . I will show them my back, not my face, on the day of their calamity." Because they want to follow their own plans, and each one of them wants to act according to the promptings of their wicked hearts.

By pointing to Jeremiah and the potter, Matthew shifts the blame away from Judas onto the religious leaders.

The evangelist Matthew (let's remember that he is a Jew, writing for Jews in Judea) apparently is making every effort to tie his brother apostle, Judas, into the divine guidance of Israel's salvation history (for which there are great models, who were known as sinners, in the history of Israel and of Jesus – just think of David [2 Sam 11]). Whatever Judas did, it happened within God's plan, which had been foretold from of old.

In that perspective, everything that happens, even the handing over of Jesus, remains enveloped in God's greater will for salvation.

That applies even more when we consider the notion of "innocent blood" (Mt 27:4).

When Judas, horrified and full of remorse, says: "I have sinned by betraying innocent blood," (exactly like this in the Greek!) this wording recalls a passage in 1 Maccabees 1:37: "On every side of the sanctuary they shed innocent blood; they even defiled the sanctuary." By this connection, Judas' action is once more enveloped in God's history of salvation with his people. After all, Deuteronomy 21:1-9 speaks of someone killed in an open field (and it is not known who killed him); the elders of the city, after they have broken the neck of a young cow, shall solemnly say: "Our hands did not shed this blood, nor were we witnesses to it. Absolve, O Lord, your people Israel, whom you redeemed; *do not let the guilt of innocent blood remain in the midst of your people Israel.*" If, with the money they have gotten from Judas, the high priests bought the field as a burial place for strangers, then (given this context) *that* for Matthew is the real crime against the will of God. Because now blood innocently shed remained in the midst of the people. Those responsible did not act according to what the Holy Scriptures demanded. The pagan, Pilate, will later act rightly, when he says: "I am innocent of this man's blood" (Mt 27:24).

In Matthew's depiction of Judas, then, we can see his effort to portray his brother apostle within God's history of salvation with his chosen people. He is not outside of it. The greater crime lies with *others*.

This is totally different from the portrayal of Judas in the history of Christianity, where, as we know, we encounter him as a traitor, responsible for Jesus' death.

This interpretation has to go. No one but Jesus, the "man of scandal" himself, is to be *blamed* (in the sense of being the cause) for his death. He knew from the start, beginning from the cleansing of the temple to his last parable, that his actions and words were contrary to the current interpretation of the Law of Moses, which was regarded as God's unsurpassable revelation. The Sanhedrin therefore had to declare that he was "deserving of death" because he was blaspheming God (Mk 14:64). Three times he fled when they wanted to stone him on the side of the road, because he wanted – and as prophet had to (see Lk 13:33) – die in Jerusalem. He wanted to give his life back into the hands of the Father at the same time as the paschal lambs were offered in the temple.

What then was the part of Judas?

Judas fulfilled the timeline, which Jesus had chosen for himself, and towards which he had directed everything.

The name Judas *Iscariot* indicates, as already mentioned, that he came from the south of Israel, from the village of Kariōt in the desert southeast of Hebron. The green landscape around the sea of Galilea was different than what he called home, and so maybe he felt a stranger there, a stranger also in the circle of fishermen as most of Jesus' other disciples were. Through their fingers ran water, through his fingers ran sand. This strangeness may have isolated him and turned him into a loner.

When Matthew mentions him for the first time in the list of the apostles, he is immediately attached with the mark of stigma: ". . . who did also deliver him up" (Mt 10:4 YLT).[12] The same for the evangelists Mark and Luke. Right from the beginning this label became permanently attached to Judas. John doesn't give us a list of apostles; but when he mentions Judas for the first time (Jn 6:70-71), he says: "He, though one of the twelve, was going to betray him." Does the added phrase "one of the twelve" mean that belonging to this chosen circle means nothing, that the same thing could happen also to any of us?

John, the evangelist, adds a little biographical note: "Judas, son of Simon Iscariot . . ." The father of our Judas is named Simon, like many men at the time. At this point Jesus

---

12. "Deliver him up" is a translation of *paradidomi*, which means "deliver," or "hand over." According to Mark 14: 44, it could be considered an "identification." In the pitch-dark night, the captors did not know which of the eleven men they were looking for.

calls his friend, Judas *diábolos*, "a devil," which at his time meant *blasphemer, slanderer*. Would he have been someone who stood out because of his blaspheming? And what would he have to blaspheme about? We don't know.

I don't think it is certain whether the term, *blasphemer*, truly goes back to Jesus himself or rather to John, because in the Gospel of John, Judas is shown in an unfavorable light. On the other hand, we cannot forget that Jesus himself called the brothers James and John "sons of thunder." One day the two of them had been very angry about the inhospitality of the Samaritans, who didn't want to provide a night's lodging for Jesus' group because they were Jews on the way to Jerusalem. In their fury, the two brothers asked Jesus for permission to let "fire come down from heaven" to destroy these people. Jesus forbade them. If then he calls them "sons of thunder" (Mk 3:17), it shows that Jesus did not shy away from more or less sharp, apt expressions.

In some older texts, it is written that Jesus added: "You don't know what spirit is speaking in you. The son of man didn't come to destroy people, but to save them."

The nickname, "sons of thunder," could also point to the fact that John, Jesus' favorite disciple and future evangelist, carried a good portion of anger and fury in him, with unbridled and unrestrained impulses. If he could not stand someone, that person didn't have a chance for the rest of their life. This could explain why Judas comes off so badly in the Gospel of John.

What prompted Judas to hand Jesus over to the Sanhedrin? Was this really only about money? Then again it is only John who tells us that Judas administered the funds of the group and misappropriated the income (Jn 12:5). This might be a fact, but it might also have been portrayed resentfully.

If the money did not play a decisive role for the handing over of Jesus, then what did?

I want to refer to a crucial scene, when James and John– those two of all people! – secretly went to Jesus asking if, once the matter of his kingdom was finally worked out, could he reserve for them the first places, on his right and on his left (Mk 10:37). This incident reveals that the other ten thought exactly like the two brothers but were indignant only because the two "sons of thunder" beat them to it, pushing to the "front of the line."

Moreover, it is clear that all twelve apostles, without exception, had a totally wrong idea of this "kingdom of God" that had been the main concern of Jesus' proclamation; they still thought of it as the "new kingdom for Israel" (Acts 1:6). Certainly, their Jesus "the Nazorean" as the whole country called him by now, was the Messiah of the house of David. He had the power to drive the evildoers and the Gentiles out of the country. If only he would finally use one of his countless opportunities to show his might and proclaim himself as the awaited Messiah! Yet he let the best occasions slip by, just like back at the lake when he healed many people and fed thousands. When the people came to proclaim him king . . . he brusquely sent everyone home.

Another incident of this kind, which Luke tells us about, must have happened in Jesus' last week in Jerusalem (Lk 13:1-9). Countless pilgrims were coming to Jerusalem for the feast, streaming into the temple (it was Jesus' last Paschal feast, in the spring of the year 30), but Galilean pilgrims along with their sacrificial animals are killed by Pilate's temple guards. Although some research casts doubt about the historicity of such an incident, Flavius Josephus does mention a similar carnage in the temple, or in Samaria, where a Galilean had been killed (*De bello Judaico* II,13; II,12:3). Therefore, Luke's account indeed seems credible to me.

Clearly, neither Judas nor the other apostles understood Jesus' reactions. In light of their compatriots being killed, they wished that he would finally shed his restraint and fight back with all his power to show that he is the Davidic Messiah. There never had been a better opportunity! The whole city was full of Jews who were only waiting for a sign from Jesus to revolt against the Romans . . . But again, Jesus declined. They wanted him to use power, just like the Romans, except that his would be even greater. If he had done this, however, in the end the cycle of power would have been perpetuated and everyone would have died just the same.

If all the apostles did reason that way, Judas was only one of the many. One could also say: all twelve, who already had been allowed the privilege of the Lord accompanying and supporting them, had also betrayed him and his mission – in their own way, in their own measure. Whether they drew practical consequences, and which ones, is another question. What exactly – and that remains to be clarified – drove Judas to hand over the Master he so greatly admired to the enemy's party?

First, note that none of the apostles, Judas included, wanted to lose Jesus! On the contrary, they needed him! Judas, just like the other eleven apostles, wanted a high position in the new kingdom of Israel and that was only possible *with* Jesus. It is very important to acknowledge this and take it into account – none of the twelve wanted Jesus' death. Surely, they were convinced that the Messiah would not die – just as the crowd that called out: "We have heard from the Law that the Messiah remains forever" (Jn 12:34). They thought that Jesus could and would prevent his own death!

Therefore, when Judas, one of the twelve, handed Jesus over to their enemies, it was by no means for the purpose that they should or would kill him! Judas must have been sure, virtually rock solid convinced, that Jesus would free himself from the hands of the enemies.

That's how much Judas trusted him!

Having been raised in the heat of the desert, perhaps Judas brought with him a different temperament than the fishermen from the coolness of the Sea of Galilee. It is entirely possible that such a plan would have matured in his mind: "Master, I will bring you into a situation in which you have to show your power. Absolutely! Otherwise, it will be over for you and your 'kingdom of God.' Then you will tell me: 'That was a clever plan, Judas! Now I will show my power!' Then I, Judas, will be famous because it was I who created the conditions for you to finally show your power before the whole world!"

Yes, perhaps Judas did come up with the plan to hand him over to the chief priests so that they could have him captured – and then everyone would see that their Jesus was truly the Messiah.

Of course, we don't really know. But some things suggest that it was like that.

Matthew's is the only book in the New Testament (apart from the Acts of the Apostles), that recounts what happened with Judas after he realized that his Master reasoned in a way altogether different from his own, from that of all the other apostles, from that of people in general. That Jesus would let himself be captured and be condemned to death; that he would renounce all power . . . – Judas would never have imagined *that*!

Matthew writes that "When Judas . . . saw that Jesus was condemned, he repented" (Mt 27:3). Judas is probably the first to regret this way of thinking, which, however, all the apostles shared. He was perhaps the first, perhaps after Mariam of Magdala and the Mother of Jesus, to realize why Jesus had become man, and what Jesus meant by saying that God makes "his sun rise on the evil and on the good . . ." (Mt 5:45).

"Jesus was innocent . . . and I am the son of destruction . . . because of me he has to die now."

"No new Israel, no kingdom of God anymore . . ."

"I have done the irreversible. No one can turn the situation around anymore . . ."

No one?

None of his friends were there to talk to him and console him and absorb the shock with him. Did his action maybe remind him of Cain, the first murderer, whom God, however, did not dismiss. Rather, the Creator himself made a sign to save him, so that no one would kill him? Neither Cain nor Judas. . .

But for God nothing is irreversible! God wants to save what is lost! And who would have been more lost than the one who handed over the Lord himself?

To have handed over the beloved Master to his death, and to be alone now, without any support, was too much for Judas to take. And now the words of Jesus, which he had heard only a few hours earlier, might have unfolded their power: "But woe to that man through whom the Son of Man is delivered up! Good it were for him if that man had not been born." And Judas – he who delivered him up – answering said, 'Is it I, Rabbi?' He saith to him, 'Thou hast said.' "(Mt 26:24-25 YLT).

When he realized what this exchange had meant, "he went and hanged himself" (Mt 27:5).

"It would have been better for that one not to have been born." How many interpretations have been drawn from this short sentence! Damnation, everlasting agony, hellish torment, no more salvation, and many similar things. Yet none of these rings out clearly in this phrase of Jesus.

Could this statement just as well be pointing to a great agony, to a going "as through fire" – to purgatory and therefore ultimately to salvation?

In the previous pages, we have witnessed Jesus' interactions with sinners, with people who are lost, far from

God. Has even one of these interactions suggested that Jesus would cast anyone for all eternity into the torments of hell? Jesus, whose name means "God saves"?

In his words and deeds, has he not revealed the true nature of his Father, who wants to save, and who will save, everyone . . . also Judas, the least of all people?

Let us not forget two insights we have gained:

First, the cause for Jesus' death was not Judas, but Jesus himself, the actions and words by which he ignored the Torah of Moses. He knew from the start that they would kill him for it, and he was prepared for it.

Second, among all his parables, which one would fit Judas? What about the one of the lost, dead, silver coin?

Out of its own initiative and willpower the coin cannot return. In fact, it has neither initiative nor willpower. Judas, his psyche having crashed into chaos, could not even beg for mercy. No one was there to help him. Only darkness and despair accompanied him. He repents and, at the same time, punishes himself. He does not see any future possibility for himself . . .

Instead, his future is *bestowed* on him. Just as the lost silver coin receives the gift of being found, he receives the gift of his future. As the lost sheep is found and carried home . . . as a gift. But at this point Judas doesn't know that.

To further explain what might have happened with Judas, I would like to return to Jesus' parable of the two lost sons. Let's look only at the second one, the older brother, and connect him with Jesus' parable of the rich glutton and the poor man, Lazarus, which Luke recounts immediately afterwards.

This older son, who day after day reliably does his work, is furious about his younger brother, this "good-for-nothing" who only needs to show up again and immediately gets a big party thrown for him! The older one becomes angry. Listen again to the father's reaction: he "came out and began to plead with him" (Lk 15:28).

Once more, we experience how God sets out to the periphery when a person struggles to go on. God is not angry, as we would be. After the son vented his anger and his sense of being treated unjustly, the father says: "Son"[*téknon*] (15:31), followed by some almost mystical words which could have been taken from Jesus' farewell speech in John: "you are always with me, and all that is mine is yours. But we had to celebrate and rejoice. . ."

Strangely enough we don't hear how the story ends; it seems as though Jesus intends to leave it unfinished. It is as though we Christians should live the end of the parable ourselves . . . Might the older son go inside in the end? If so, what will he do? Will he have his festive meal outside? The parable ends with "we had to celebrate and rejoice" (15:32).

Only four chapters later, Luke presents another of Jesus' parables – the one about the rich glutton and the poor Lazarus (Lk 16:19-31). There are good reasons to assume that Jesus gave a historic name to the main person in this story. It is the only time in all his parables that he names a character in a parable, and he used the name of his friend, Lazarus, the brother of Martha and Mary, to give tribute to him for all eternity.

It is a parable about Hades, purgatory, "heavenly rehab." The story is well-known, but it contains two facts that are little known, or not at all. They are wonderful, incredible! Inexplicable.

There is the rich self-absorbed man. He lives arrogantly, indulging in pleasures. Other people do not exist for him. Outside his door lies Lazarus, covered in sores, hungry. Only the dogs come and lick his wounds. He dies and he comes into Abraham's bosom, into heaven, so to say (because in the Hebrew word for bosom also echoes the word "mercy").

The materialistic egocentric man dies, too, and he comes into *Hades,* into the netherworld (not hell!). It is purgatory. We shall see now why we may absolutely and more appropriately call it "heavenly rehab." In the (metaphorical) fire, he suffers great agony and pain, and maybe he thinks to himself: "If only I would have never been born . . . Couldn't Lazarus at least bring me some water?" But Abraham denies it to him.

And now something unheard-of and wonderful happens. The rich egotist pleads with Abraham to send Lazarus to his father's house, where five other brothers live, obviously being just as egocentric as he had been. They should be warned, so that they won't have to come to this place of agony . . . What is happening here? For the first time the self-centered man thinks of others! The agony, the pain in this "rehab" have melted his shell. He begins to think of others – at least they should be warned so they will not have to come here!

What does Jesus tell us here?

For God, our death is not a final deadline by which a person's definitive decision must be made. No, God works for each human person also beyond death. What they did not understand and do during their life, they must understand and do the hard way now, under pain and suffering. The rich egotist does not at all, as our tradition always has said, go to hell without any redemption. Not at all! He, too, shall be saved. It is God's nature to save, but "as through fire," to be re-melted and transformed, if the egotist failed to do so here on earth, through the many chances that life offered. Even that one will grow in the capacity to love.

How then should we understand Jesus' statement: "It would have been better for that one not to have been born . . ."? Of course, the agony undergone in this "rehab" makes a person think many times: "If only I had . . ., if only . . ., if I would not have . . . then I would not have needed to suffer this pain now!"

Yet without the pain and the suffering, transformation cannot come about.

Yes, even the rich glutton will be saved, but "as through fire." The first sign of his becoming a "new creation" is that he thinks of his five brothers. Could it be that Jesus here gives us a hint of how the parable of the second lost son might have ended? How the younger one could have brought the older, stubborn brother into the banquet hall after all? Could it be the younger brother who thinks of the older one and goes out towards him?

Do I have to go out again and again to the one who cannot or who does not want to come . . .?

And Judas? Is he really the only one who will not be saved, to whom no one reaches out to console him in his "rehab," to tell him that the Master, through his death, carried the sins of the whole world? Doesn't it hold true also for him: "You will be transformed and created new, even though you need to undergo agony and pain?"

If none of the twelve climbs down from heaven into the netherworld where Judas is undergoing transformation – his mother surely will!

Because there is something else, a wonderful discovery. A mysterious coincidence? At least something that I cannot explain.

Not long ago, when I read this parable again, slowly, and attentively, I suddenly realized that Abraham calls the rich egotist, "child" (Lk 16:25). It made me stop. I had read that word before; it was mentioned also somewhere else in the Gospels. To whom else had Jesus said this word . . .? And then, I found it right away. It was in the parable of the two lost sons, directly before that, in which the father says the exact same word to the older son: "*téknon*[my child]" (15:31). Abraham addresses the egotist to be purified in the fire with the very same word: "*téknon*[my child]."

But I also discovered something else. In the parable of the lost sons, the father of the two sons goes out to the stubborn and hardheaded one . . . He goes out to him! Is the word "my child" in a theological-divine way linked to the fact that God is not able to say this word without going towards the one to whom he says it? Because with God, his word never goes out without a deed. Thus, in this word of Abraham to the egotist in the fire of the netherworld, we can hear expressed a divine movement towards the person. When God says, "My child," he goes out to this person. Even into the fire.

Now the observation of the mysterious: When I looked at the parable of poor Lazarus and the rich glutton, simply looked at it with my eyes, I suddenly felt that the word "my child" stood somehow in the center. Yes, quite in the middle . . . I smiled – and then I did something that maybe not everyone does! I took the Greek text and counted, counted from the beginning of the parable up to the word "*téknon*" – it was the 122nd word. And then I counted after this word to the end of the parable – and it was 122 words . . .

"*Téknon*[my child]" stands exactly in the center.

I can't explain that.

Did Luke arrange that or Jesus himself?

It is a mystery. The mystery that with God the one who is lost is at the center. As his child. The lost one, the stubborn one is the target of his divine movement, down into the transforming fire. In the center of the Good News of the cleansing purgatory, lifting everything that seems irreversible, stands this word, "my child." While he says it, God moves towards human persons, no matter where they stand and what they want.

And Judas?

The last "word" that Jesus uses to address his apostle is "my friend." It is an expression of familiar relationship similar to "my child." With this word of affection from the Son of God, Judas dies. His body hangs on a tree, but his soul hangs on this word of loving attention: "my friend!"

What God, the Eternal, has said once, holds true for all eternity. It holds true also in the hereafter, in purgatory as well as in glory. And when Judas arrives for the "judgment" – and judgment for God means to be saved – then the first thing he hears is this eternal word, "my friend," which will transform him, will turn everything around. "As through fire."

Because God goes out to him and carries him to his place at the heavenly banquet.

Maybe the heavenly Father gives us time, so that one of us might go out to console and encourage someone, telling them that the love of God cannot be destroyed.

Yes, it is not only Abraham who is the "friend of God." God also called Judas, the one who wanted to urge the Master to finally show his power "friend," so that he may realize, so that the whole world may realize, that God's power consists in his love. God's love cannot be stopped by death or any guilt, however great it may be – whether the sinner admits to it here on earth or not. Yes, his power is in his transforming mercy, which he also, and especially, wants to bestow on those who are *bad*.

I want to give to the last as much as to the first!

The secret of the "Good Shepherd of Vézelay"

The "stream" of 2000 years of tradition has flooded millions of Christians again and again with catechism phrases stating that Jesus was the "victim" of their fault and their sins, that he died virtually as the "sacrifice" for their irredeemable offenses, so that through his death God would be "reconciled" and his anger appeased.

We may ask how many people have felt deeply ashamed by such a theology and have suffered in their spiritual/psychological health because of it – totally against God's intentions!

It is an agony to be told over and over that God offered himself for my sake, because I am so bad, because I am a failure . . . If then, according to this way of thinking, God nonetheless makes himself the "victim" (or rather, if it is interpreted like that), it cannot lead the person to a true transformation. It cannot promote healing, but only a lasting attrition. Yet, many Christians of every century have been educated and kept in bondage with precisely these accusatory tactics. To say it a little drastically, we could define it as religious psychological torture. It is education through the principles of fear and guilt, always repeating this message alone: "You should be ashamed!" These are firmly cemented

Visitors and pilgrims looking at the capital of the Good Shepherd of Vézelay

in formulas, like in the confession of our sins. We say *"Mea culpa, mea culpa, mea maxima culpa . . ."* – "through my fault, through my fault, through my most grievous fault."

Instead, on the other side of Christian tradition, we have that wonderful text of the *Exsultet* at the Easter Vigil, focused totally on the reality of our salvation: "O happy fault, which gained for us so great a Redeemer!" Redeemer! Not: "What great a sacrifice you demanded!"

The topics of sin and sacrifice have been placed much too far in the forefront. Because of that, in my opinion in many believers a true joyful faith could not develop, in the sense of a joyful relationship with God. The critics of religion have found fault with this again and again, throughout the centuries, since such a victim-centered and guilt-ridden theology virtually *had* to lead them to the conclusion that religion oppresses and makes believers sick. Somehow, they are not all that wrong in their critique.

A theology dominated by "sin and fault" has obscured the decisive message that God loves us out of his own free will (!); the Good News that he carries everyone home, especially the sinner and the least, and that *he gives himself personally (!) for each one, out of love.* That is why many have remained "servants" and did not become "friends" . . . That, however, is not the message of Jesus!

Reflecting such an accusatory and condemning theology of sacrifice and guilt, in the Church of St. Lazarus, in Autun, we have the depiction of Judas hanging by a rope on a tree, awaiting hell, with the "two demons beneath him hungrily craving their prey."

But there is another Judas, in the Church in Vézelay, who is being saved by the Good Shepherd himself.

At the beginning of this book, we looked at this picture, the work of the unknown sculptor in Vézelay, completed nearly 900 years ago. On the capital immediately on the right in the front of the basilica, the Good Shepherd is depicted carrying the dead Judas home on his shoulders. At that time, such a thing was a theological scandal because Judas belonged in hell, as it is depicted at St. Lazarus in Autun. But in Vézelay, in the Basilica of St. Mary Magdalene, an artist had secretly reasoned against every tradition and listened to his heart.

The conclusion of the thoughts of his heart he literally hid, high up in the dark – and until now evidently no one had discovered his secret.

On the contrary, there is a beautiful, official book about this church and its countless capitals, in full color and beautifully rendered *(Vézelay: une Bible de pierre*, 2010*)*. And the heading for this one with its wonderful depiction, is of all things: *Le suicide de Judas*[The suicide of Judas] . . .

But what is it that we see in the image? Isn't the primary message here that Judas is being carried home by his Lord? In the center stands the Good Shepherd carrying the dead Judas on his shoulders! Yet contrary to everything that one can see and nearly reach with one's hand, in the stone-like immobility of traditional diction it says: "*The suicide of Judas . . .*"

It is true that one needs to look for a long time to discover the extraordinary truth that the sculptor revealed here. He hid the thoughts of his heart, and only in our century are we able to see it. And we can do so only by looking at the depiction and meditating on it for a long, long time.

I am fortunate enough to have a large and clear reproduction of it on the wall in my study, dominating the entire room. I can look at it and think about it all the time. Time and again, my eyes have been attracted to the shepherd's face . . .

Until one day something caught my eye. The face of the shepherd looks like it is divided in two. The left side of his face, meaning the right one for us who are facing it, seems to be depicted normally; yes, it even seems to show a soft smile. While the lower right half of the shepherd's face appears to be lifeless, flat, as though untouched, as though the sculptor forgot to show his art also here. It's impossible that it was an oversight because the man had an enormous talent to bring stone to life, as the other capitals and also this one sufficiently show – one only needs to look at the face of the hanged Judas right next to it. Such a "mistake" with the face of the shepherd could not have happened.

And yet the right side of Jesus' face looks untouched. The shepherd's mouth in particular seems to be virtually cut in half. The right side of the mouth, different from the left, is almost nonexistent.

It gives Jesus' face a serious and melancholy appearance.

My curiosity was awakened. A mistake? An oversight? I could exclude that. Did the artist mean to say something through this flat, unfinished face? But what?

It took me weeks. In the meantime, I had received small photos of this picture. With those I could do something I wasn't able to do with the big picture on the wall – something that throughout the centuries no one, really no one, could have done with the capital up there in the dark: I could turn the picture upside down and take a "new" look at it.

There was a clear reason for this. Judas' head is hanging off the shepherd's left shoulder, therefore it is upside down, "standing on its head." I wanted to see this head in the correct perspective, to see what the dead Judas looked like. I turned the little photo around – and nearly got a fright. This face of Judas, who is being carried home, shows a smile. Unmistakable! He smiles! As though everything has turned out well. It is an almost blissful, soft smile, subdued and yet obvious. Wonderful.

The dead Judas smiles! As though he were not dead . . . as though everything had been turned around . . .

Felix culpa – blessed fault. Here it became visible!

As though he had experienced and heard his Master in the judgment already, as though he hears Jesus calling him for the second time, "my friend."

Yes, I want to be your friend – for all eternity.

Time and again I looked at the smiling, redeemed Judas. Oh, that felt good, to see him so redeemed!

After I had closely looked at him for long enough, I noticed something else, something very normal, very natural.

Since Jesus carried Judas over his shoulder, with his legs to the right, then on the left, above his shoulder, had to be his head hanging down. The result is that one can see only the right half of Judas' face. The left half disappears between the shoulder and the arm of the shepherd.

The right half of the face . . .

For a moment I did not dare to continue the thought . . .

That was the part that seems to be unfinished in the face of Jesus. With him only the left half of the face was developed, with Judas only the right . . .

Did they belong together?

Was it only together that they make up the whole face?

And so, I took the liberty to do what in earlier centuries could not have been done. I carefully cut out the visible lower half of Judas' face and put it on the "missing" lower right half of the shepherd's face . . .

It is *one* face!

The measurements are perfectly exact.

And now, now the good shepherd *laughs*!

Now Jesus laughs!

When I was able to do this, I saw that, with the help and with the – as he is called – greatest of all sinners, God laughs.

You, dear readers, can follow the process of this theology from the heart of the sculptor through the pictures on the following pages.

God can laugh only when the last and the greatest of all sinners has become one with him. God wants to laugh with our face, and we shall laugh with the divine face. When Peter the Venerable writes to Heloise about Abelard that he may be "embraced instead of by you, by God in love, as your other self," we may say that of Judas, too: "Embrace him as my other self."

With God, there are no outcasts.

He carries all home and transforms their tears into laughter.

Epilogue

Dear reader,

You have arrived at the ending of this book. Yet, it is not over, it continues. Its six editions in German-speaking countries have prompted many readers to write letters of gratitude, but some also had questions for which they did not find an answer in the book. Therefore, I have gathered the questions and problems mentioned to me into eight categories of topics and tried to address them and find an answer. My publisher in Germany was open to producing them as a separate little booklet, but here in the American edition we want to incorporate them directly in this book.

Should you have new questions that have not yet been addressed, please send them to the New City Press Publishing house. I am looking forward to them, and if possible, will answer them.

Fr. Christoph Wrembek, S.J.

Questions
and Answers

What about
repentance and conversion?

Q1: If, in the end, there will be unconditional redemption for everyone, are you saying that repentance and conversion are of no importance for attaining divine salvation?

A: In the fifteenth chapter of Luke's Gospel, we find the three parables of "lost ones," in which Jesus clearly suggests that the heavenly Father does not want anyone to be lost. But someone might object, "Are repentance and conversion not conditions for attaining salvation?"

Let us have a closer look. In the story of the "lost son" (see Luke 15 . . .), we still detect some "repentance and conversion," although, ultimately it is more the survival instinct, his hunger, that pushes him toward conversion. He has squandered everything and has suffered terrible misery. However, the return itself seems to transform him internally: there is no more mention of his desire for the food the hired workers receive. The father acknowledges the son's return with joy; he does not want to see him crushed and full of remorse. Rather, he wants to be one with him. He seals this communion with a feast. For Jesus whatever conversation might have taken place between father and son is literally "not worth mentioning." God simply wants to celebrate with him now that he has been found.

In the parable of the "lost sheep," Jesus shows us the Father's attitude even more clearly. We can assume some sort of "repentance," since the little sheep was crying *bitterly* for help, but that was probably out of sheer fear. It was impossible for it to return to the flock. The Good Shepherd had to set out to save it. If Jesus speaks later about a sinner who *returned*, he did not return "on his own two feet," but rather on the shoulders of the shepherd who carried the "little sheep" home.

We see a further step in the parable of the "lost coin," where everything is completely left up to God. He personally takes the whole return upon himself, simply because he wants to save. The lost coin can neither repent nor convert, nor even show fear – it is dead. At the height of the parable, the Son of God makes it clear that the less a person is able to contribute to salvation by themselves, the more God will do, because he is Love. The created being does not first need to earn and pay for this love. Love is always given in advance. Only in business dealings do we ask for deposits and trade with each other. But God is not a businessman; he is not out to gain anything to his own advantage and satisfaction. Being wise he knows that conversion and repentance often happen only after (undeserved) redemption, because of insight and gratitude.

Just think that even nonbelievers (maybe they actually **are** believers, but not inserted in the structures of the Church) save other people without laying down any conditions. They risk their lives because saving someone makes sense. Just think of the doctors, nurses, police officers, firefighters, and healthcare personnel during the COVID-19 pandemic. Should God's love be less? Less love than what countless people show us by their selfless example?

In my interpretation of the "parable of the rich glutton and the poor man, Lazarus" (see pages 114 - 119), I point out how "repentance and conversion" can also happen *after* our life here on earth.

It is only in the fire of Hades (in the glowing fire of God's love, since there is no other fire) that the rich glutton comes to his senses and is open to being transformed . . . and ready to think of others.

For the eternal God, who created time and eternity, our death is not a border that, once crossed, ends his possibility to act. I am convinced that God continues to work at our salvation, also after we have died, by giving us the chance *after* our death to think clearly and therefore recognize our own wrong behavior, by showing himself to us directly. Faced with the most sublime beauty and goodness and truth of God, how could even the least penitent sinner refuse?

At this point, every person will come to know God, as well as themselves. Faced with the eternal goodness of God, he or she, painfully aware, will repent of their omissions and instead long for God infinitely. It is our sure hope that everyone will be received in the fullness of this love.

Conversion and repentance, yes, are *necessary*. It is good and makes sense to live with this attitude here on earth (to the degree that it is possible!). It is good to express our sincere effort to grow in love, to show what we would like to be, and to act by the measure of God's love.

If someone does not do this, for whatever reason they are prevented from doing so, our good Lord is not going to let them fail, for eternity, because of their stupidity or stubbornness or arrogance. Even if the person's incapacity is caused perhaps by inner dullness or exhausted desperation, there is still hope.

Doesn't God forgive even before we repent? Isn't it true that we can repent only because he has already accepted us?

God will open the eyes of each one of us. For God who is all powerful Love, there are no boundaries or conditions.

The freedom
of the human person

Q2: What about the freedom of the human person?

Is God's omnipotence limited by the encounter with our freedom? Or does our freedom, given to us by God, cease to exist in the face of God's omnipotence? If Judas in his freedom has distanced himself from God, doesn't God have to respect that? So then, is there condemnation?

A: It seems to me that the relationship between human freedom and God's freedom is *the* decisive mark on our journey toward God, the moment when we are truly "freed" and with infinite trust, gaze at God's infinite possibilities. He is the eternal One, the inexpressible One. He is God who wants to transform everyone and everything into Goodness, leading all to their fulfillment.

But does God constrain anyone who does not want to be with him? If we are not free to decide against God, would we not be puppets without free will? Wouldn't all life then be meaningless?

Or are things altogether different?

Maybe the intermingling of limited human freedom with God's omnipotent freedom could be explained with a modern parable:

There is a fly in Memphis; in its fly-freedom it has decided to fly to Chicago. It heads northward, finds an opening, and flies aboard an Amtrak train. Inside the train it keeps heading north. Nothing and no one obstruct its freedom; it makes its way through the train's compartments, past the doors and past the sandwiches, constantly flying north. When the doors of the Amtrak train open it flies out – and finds itself in New Orleans. In all its north-pointing freedom, the fly's destination has been enveloped by and subsumed into the "dimension of the Amtrak," without disregarding or erasing the fly's freedom. The "dimension of the train" has integrated the "dimension of the fly," and so it arrived in a "different world."

Such higher "dimension-worlds" surround us in ever new levels. We walk towards the west, but the earth turns east. Our freedom to walk west is not taken away or disregarded by the earth rotating east, but it is surrounded or integrated into a higher, greater dimension. Or take this example: the earth moves around the sun – but our solar system, our Milky Way, moves the sun and the stars, the human person and the fly included, in an altogether different direction. How many dimensions are there? Some astrophysicists say eleven, or more!

The last, all-encompassing dimension is what we call God. God "integrates," subsumes our freedom in his all-embracing movement of loving mercy.

Our human freedom, and the many dimensions beyond it, are all enveloped by divine freedom – that is a great mystery, for which our words are inadequate.

If we look at what we call "freedom," we must admit that, by today's knowledge, it has many limitations and conditions. The human person is not as free as he or she believes. Every person, in various ways, is shaped by their origins, upbringing, nationality, culture, education (or lack, thereof)... and religion. We are influenced by our past and by the countless people in our life – in short, by our complex past and present. There are individual aspects of which we might not even be aware, which shape us and our "free" decisions in great measure. Recent psychological and neuro-physiological research supports these insights, and theological discussions cannot avoid them.

At the same time, the future can also shape us, with its fears or opportunities, its dreams and attractions.

Both the past and the future influence us and our conscience, influence us in significant measure in our *free* choices and self-determination. We need to become aware, bit by bit, of how embedded and dependent we are. Through earnest exchange with others who are more mature, we can develop deeper insights about ourselves and the world around us. Only then can we widen the small space of the freedom we have to control our life.

Given this background, we do not begin with questions about fault and failure or even allegedly self-inflicted punishment. Rather, it is often the case that I simply need the help and support of others. Has not everyone, at times, "fallen among thieves"?

If someone has caused a serious accident by speeding carelessly and now lies severely injured on the road, the first responders will not ask: "Do you want to be helped?" The person would hardly answer: "No, I don't want help!"

Or, if someone is standing on a windowsill, intending to jump, he or she is *free* to do that, but the rescuers will not first ask: "Do we have permission to save you?" Strangely enough, *rescuing* someone always takes precedence over the *freedom* to destroy oneself.

From God's point of view, the human person is like someone seriously injured on the side of the road, like someone who has fallen among thieves . . .

In certain cases, the courts decide that the perpetrator of a crime was not of *sound mind*. We may ask if Judas was of sound mind. Or did the many influences from his past (and his wishes for the future) make him not all that *free*? One thing is certain: Judas surely did not want the death of Jesus. He needed Jesus (and so did the other disciples) to fulfill the dream of a privileged place in his kingdom! Judas only wanted to maneuver Jesus into a position that would force him finally to show his power. He was compelled by that idea which therefore may have guided his so-called *free* decision.

How, then, does a human being's *free* decision work? The human person, it seems to me, in his or her conditioned freedom, decides always for what seems to be *better* in that moment, what is more desirable, more beautiful, possibly more opportune, more enjoyable and, in various ways, more *profitable*. This may be wrong in the long run. It may be wrong objectively, but *now, in this moment,* it seems best.

Personal freedom therefore is always attracted by, and freely wants to have, whatever *in that moment* seems to be better, more beautiful, more profitable, or more desirable – no matter what damage it might provoke for oneself or for others.

By being drawn to this "something which is so attractive," is the person then not free? No, one could say in modern terms that it reflects the way we are programmed by our Creator: namely, always wanting what seems better or more beautiful *now*. (In technical terms, it is described in Latin as *sub respectu boni*, meaning "under the appearance of good.")

However, what seems *concretely* better or more beautiful is, all too often, only the more opportune, what is most important to *me*, more enjoyable or advantageous in the short term – without considering the consequences for me and for others.

Here on earth, we human beings are attracted by what is "beautiful"; one can be captivated by beauty, or even more by greater financial gain. And so on. Even if I decide against "beauty," I remain within the scope of my freedom: I decide what to me seems better than beauty.

If the human person stands before God, then God is, as we say, the *summum Bonum- Pulchrum-Verum,* the utmost Good, Beautiful and True – and there is no alternative besides God, because God is Infinite Being! This means that everything that ever seemed beautiful, good, true, or desirable in life is contained in the Absolute God, freed of what is relative and short-term, transformed and exceeded a million times. Then our freedom will want this, yes, even *need* to want this. How could it be different, since our freedom is always directed toward what seems good-true-beautiful, in order to fulfill ourselves.

In other words, our freedom is *attracted* to God! God is so *attractive* that the created being *needs* to want HIM! "And I, when I am lifted up from the earth, will draw [attract] all people to myself. . ." (Jn 12:32), Jesus says. Is the human person's freedom taken away by that? No, on the contrary! This is its fulfillment, to obtain what it has been yearning for, and has always wanted.

When Mary Magdalene came to the house of Simon the Pharisee with the alabaster jar, she was free – free to do what? Free to leave again? Nonsense! She was attracted by this man, Jesus. Her freedom found its fulfillment in being and remaining with this person. That is how it will be with us when we stand before God: in God, our freedom finds its fulfillment and completion.

I love to quote Edith Stein[13] in this context. She writes: *"Human freedom cannot be broken by the divine, nor suppressed, but it can be outwitted, as it were. The descent of Grace into the human soul is a free act of divine love. And there are no limits to its expansion."*[14]

Let us not forget: God is free, God is the infinitely Eternal One. The savior and redeemer! *His* freedom is the only true and absolute freedom in which everything and everyone – in a way still hidden from us – will come to fulfilment according to *God's* good will.

---

13. Edith Stein, 1891 – 1942, philosopher and spiritual writer who converted from Judaism to Catholicism. Baptized in 1922, she became a Discalced Carmelite nun and took on the religious name of Teresa Benedicta of the Cross. Because of her Jewish ancestry she was executed by the Nazis in Auschwitz. Edith Stein is regarded a modern martyr. She was declared a saint by the Roman Catholic Church in 1998 and is one of the six co-patron Saints of Europe.

14. Edith Stein, „Freiheit und Gnade" und weitere Beiträge zu Phänomenologie und Ontologie: (1917 bis 1937) (Freiburg: Herder, 2014), 158 -59. Our translation.

Damnation: an article of faith?

Q3: Is damnation part of the Christian belief? Did God not reveal everlasting pain in hell for all those who remain stubborn and sinful until the end?

A: History is full of terrible atrocities – people are capable of inflicting inconceivable pain on each other. Even supposedly "just" punishments can be of unspeakable horror. Often it all seems to be more about revenge than atonement and purification. In the case of great guilt, it is often simply about annihilating the perpetrator(s). Is that how we imagine God to be? Someone who makes culprits suffer everlasting agonies in the fires of hell? Didn't God say to Jeremiah that such a thing (casting people into fire) would never come to his mind (Jer 32:35)?

The term "damnation"[15] is not found in the "Subject Indexes" of the substantial descriptions of our Catholic faith, and yet, it is argued, we do find the term "hell," and therefore indirectly also "damnation." Or not?

To offer a clarifying summary, we can look one more time into the original texts of our Holy Scriptures. Back then, there was no word for what we today understand as

---

15. The term is found neither in the subject register of the Catechism of the Catholic Church, nor in Joseph Ratzinger's *Introduction to Christianity*. It speaks for itself that versions of the Apostles' Creed in languages other than English nor the Nicene Creed use that term. Damnation doesn't have an important place in the faith of the Catholic Church, and even more, the idea that people would be damned is not part of the belief of the Catholic Church.

"hell," neither in the Greek nor in the Hebrew. The New Testament, therefore, never speaks of "hell"! In the accounts of the evangelists Jesus uses three terms: *Hades, Gehenna* and *Abyssus*. None of these terms denotes "hell" *as* we understand it today. Consequently, it is wrong to translate them as "hell."

After the Second Vatican Council, the term "hell" in the Apostles' Creed has been eliminated in many languages (not in English) and replaced with "netherworld" – a correction long overdue, as Greek and Latin scholars have known for centuries. If some authors, even those who are quite renowned, still use "hell," it remains incorrect. *"Descendit ad infernos"* means "descended into the netherworld," which is a world apart from the meaning of "hell." The Old Testament says that with God's help and power one can return from the netherworld. The netherworld (like our "purgatory") serves for a person's purification. It aims at the salvation of the sinner, a preparation for the entrance into the kingdom of God's Love.

That leads, according to me, to a powerful consequence. If, after the Second Vatican Council, this linguistic error was corrected, it should be necessary to correct the countless misinterpretations of theology made throughout history, all of which are connected to this incorrect translation. Now that the former term "hell" has been, etymologically, substituted, and rightly so, by the term "netherworld," shouldn't this term be used in texts of all the various synods, councils, and promulgations over the years? They all should use "netherworld" instead of "hell." To me that seems logical.

If someone were to ask why God has permitted such mistakes for so long, we should first ask ourselves why *we* have not started to think critically, to question and come to a better understanding of these concepts. The human person, sadly, listens less to God than to themselves. Holy Scriptures are inspired by God, but at the same time are written by human beings. Inevitably, the so-called revelations always contain remnants of their contemporary culture, which are necessarily tied to their historic times. The challenge is always to "sense" the core, the essence of God's being, beyond the written work of human hands. The Spirit of God will lead us more and more into the truth (see Jn 16:13), as we may hope, trusting in Jesus' promise. We are called to go deeper and deeper in our understanding – in the present context of each age.

This places a controversial topic at the center of the Church – I am aware of that. Is it truly a loss if we call into question many old "certain" truths? It may disturb the thinking of many, but does it not require *greater* faith to trust that God's Spirit is capable of revealing, in our present time, new dimensions of the Good News?

In addition to all this, Jesus, our Lord, was not afraid of controversy. He was completely attentive to the "truth" of his Father, and he had the courage to bear witness to it – even if it cost him his life. To follow this Jesus with all our strength, with our best knowledge and conscience, *that* is – faithfulness.

"Hell" in the Bible

Q4: The Bible speaks of "everlasting fire," where there is "wailing and grinding of teeth." Isn't that an unmistakable description of hell and eternal damnation?

A: As I explained in this book, the passages that mention "everlasting fire" are (almost) exclusively found in Matthew. Therefore, one has to consider why the other Gospels don't use this terminology. We would expect them to do so if they were truly Jesus' words. Therefore, did they enter Matthew's Gospel for some other reason? Did they come not from Jesus, but rather from his opponents? The latter seems to be the case, since these figures of speech, typical of Jewish-apocalyptic literature of his times, differ from the message of Jesus in significant ways.[16]

Furthermore, the word "everlasting" needs to be considered. Matthew uses the word *aiōn* exclusively, which means "a long time." The other word *aïdios* is used only by Paul (Rm 1:20), to mean "eternity," in today's understanding. The "everlasting fire" (in Matthew) is, therefore, not everlasting. It only lasts quite a long time. In Matthew 13:39-40 it says that the harvest is the end of the *aiōnos* – which NRSV translates as "the end of the age." Here too, it is referring to a timeframe in the *world*. And there are many such places. Conclusion: wherever we read "eternal" we

---

16. How they entered into the Gospel of Matthew (and only into *his* Gospel!) I have tried to explain in my book *Sentire Jesum* (available only in German).

ought, in the light of the Greek, to verify what is intended. The "everlasting fire" in the Gehinnom valley is referring to the garbage dump of Jerusalem, which will smolder for a long time.

Let's recap. Nowhere does God's revelation in the New Testament speak of "hell" as some understand it today. For the God of mercy and of all consolation who wants to save everyone, there is neither damnation nor a gruesome place where there would be an everlasting fire burning. If that be the case, then we might as well, drastically speaking, forget about our faith. It would not be understandable why the Palestinian Jews at that time would have called Jesus' message "the *Good* News." Even if, once we are in front of God, a painful transformation process will have to happen, we cannot forget that God's aim is salvation and redemption!

Redemption for all?

Q5: What about God's "redemption for all"? Does that mean that every evil person and every scoundrel will go to heaven?

A: Among theologians there is a burning discussion around this topic of *apocatastasis*.[17] I will not get into this here. I also do not want to oppose declarations made by the Church; they remain valid. I know that Hans Urs von Balthasar risked his neck with this topic, and later on was made a Cardinal. In the context of a clean, plausible argument, drawing from Holy Scriptures and from the findings of the great mystics, Von Balthasar ventured to say that in the face of the infinite love of God, we may at least *hope* that in the end hell will be empty.[18]

---

17. Greek *apocatastasis*, Latin restitution in *pristinum statum*, meaning "restoration to the original condition." This is the name given in the history of theology to the doctrine that teaches that a time will come when all free creatures will share in the grace of salvation, in a special way the devils and the lost souls. Traditional theology speaks of "devils," whereas the original Greek does not know this word or has a different understanding of it than we have today. The same with "lost souls" which refers to a traditional thinking, but today's theology knows that there are no lost souls for the eternal God of love, who has come to save the whole world (see Jn 12,47).

18. Regarding the thought that *in the end* even the worst criminals shall be with God, difficult for our imagination, see page 156.

I will limit myself to a few passages in the New (and Old) Testament which could serve as evidence for the possibility of redemption for all.

Jesus uses the image from the great Old Testament prophet Isaiah when he speaks of the eschatological wedding banquet on Mount Zion where "*all* peoples" will sit at the heavenly banquet and enjoy the best wine and the finest food (Is 25:6-7). *All* peoples! It does not say that first they must show repentance, conversion, and penance. Jesus, our Lord, picks up this image when he describes the royal wedding banquet (Mt 22:1-10), where *all* will be called together again, from the street corners and along the roads, *all*, the bad and the good. Does not Jesus, the Savior of humankind, also say: "And I, when I am lifted up from the earth, will draw all people to myself" (Jn 12:32)? Does not Paul pick up this word, when he says, "Christ Jesus . . . gave himself a ransom *for all*" (1Tm 2:6)? In another place, it says that the God and Father of all decided to "gather up all things in him [Christ], things in heaven and things on earth" (Eph 1:10). Our salvation rings out most profoundly in the well-known passage of the letter to the Romans: "For God has imprisoned all in disobedience so that he may be merciful to *all*" (Rm 11:32). "For the grace of God has appeared, bringing salvation to *all*" (Ti 2:11). These passages may prove that there is a good foundation to speak of the divine will to bring about *apocatastasis* – salvation for all.

But Judas? Does that hold true also for him? Judas stands for the least of all people, the lowest of all sinners. For many he is the *condemned par excellence*. Here I find consolation in Jesus' clear words: "I choose to give to this last one the same as I give to you!" (Mt 20:14).

As I mentioned, Hans Urs von Balthasar cites words of Edith Stein (declared a saint on November 11, 1998) regarding this topic. I would like to mention here some other passages of the saint:

It is not enough to consider freedom by itself. One must also examine what Grace can accomplish, and whether there are any absolute limits to it. We have already seen that Grace must come to human beings. At best, human beings can reach the door, but no one can force their entry. Furthermore, Grace can come to them, without their searching, without their willing. The question is whether Grace can accomplish its work without the cooperation of [human] freedom.

Edith Stein, too, is convinced that grace can come to a person without him or her searching for it. But we can go even further than Edith Stein. If you permit, I want to remind you that the risen Jesus did not only come "up to the gate," but he entered through locked doors!

Edith Stein further writes:

All-merciful love can descend upon anyone. We believe that it does. And now, should there be souls who exclude themselves from it permanently? In principle, the possibility is not excluded. In fact, it can become i n f i n i t e l y   u n l i k e l y [!], precisely through what prevenient Grace is able to accomplish in the soul. This Grace can only knock, and there are souls that open themselves at even this quiet call. Others let it go unheeded. But then this Grace can worm its way into these souls, and more and more expand itself in them. The greater the space that it occupies in such an "illegitimate way, the more unlikely it will be that the soul closes itself off. It already sees the world now in the light of grace . . .

The more ground that Grace wins from that which occupied it before, the more ground it deprives from the free acts directed against it. And, in principle, there are no limits to this displacement. When all the impulses against the spirit of light are displaced from the soul, then a free decision against it [the spirit of light] *becomes infinitely unlikely. For this reason, the belief in the boundlessness of God's love and Grace, as well as the hope for universal salvation, are justified. . .*

Which paths divine Grace chooses for its activity, why it courts one soul, and lets another soul court it, if and how and when it is active where our eyes do not notice any of its workings; these are all questions that elude rational penetration.[19]

---

19. Edith Stein, „*Freiheit und Gnade*" *und weitere Beiträge zu Phänomenologie und Ontologie: (1917 bis 1937)* (Freiburg: Herder, 2014), 158 -59. Our translation.

The "son of destruction"?

Q6: Judas is called the "son of destruction" in John's Gospel, and in Matthew's Gospel Jesus says that it would be better for him had he never been born. Does that not clearly state eternal damnation for Judas, as also many Fathers of the Church have understood it?

A: In the original text of John 17:12 we find the word *apōleias*, which sometimes is translated as "doomed to or headed to destruction." If one looks at John's whole sentence, one cannot but be confused, because the evangelist writes, ". . . and not one of them was lost [*apōleto*] except the one destined to be lost [*apōleias*]. . ." [20] John, therefore, uses the same Greek word (derived from *apollymi*), in one place translated with "lost" – and immediately afterwards with "destruction." In fact, *apollymi* can have different meanings: perish, ruin, destroy, lose, get lost, and others. Although some translations reflect that John uses the same word for both, many do not.

Is the translation "son of 'destruction'" the only possible one that suggests itself here? How should we understand that it would be better for a person "not to have been born"? Is there only one possible interpretation?

At least a doubt would be appropriate here. For our word "destruction," the Greek also uses other terms: such as *phthōra*, *diaphthōra*, *olethros*. If John now chooses exactly

---

20. The Greek actually states it more precisely: "No one was lost except the Son of Forlornness."

the same word *apōleias* that he had used six words before (*apōleto*), translated as "lost," should one not carefully reason and wonder whether a translation as "destruction" could really be correct? Maybe John wanted to express something different?

The word *apollymi* appears, in fact, quite frequently in the New Testament. Four (out of ninety-one) passages can be of interest to us here:

– In Luke, the "lost sheep" is characterized with the exact same word: *apōlesas, apōlolos*. The lost sheep receives the same description as Judas! (Or the other way around?)

– We find the same word for the "lost coin": *apōlesa*! It certainly is not the "coin of destruction."

– Now it is hardly surprising that the father in the parable calls the son whom he had lost: *apōlolos*! "For this son of mine was dead, and is alive again, he was *lost* and is found . . ." (Lk 15:24). We would not speak here of the "son of destruction"!

Let us look then at one more passage in John's Gospel: "A thief comes only to steal and kill and destroy [*apolesē*]. I came so that they might have life and have it abundantly." (Jn 10:10). A thief wants to destroy! But God?

It seems to me that this strongly suggests that we should not translate the passage in John 17:12 as son of "destruction," and then take this into account in the interpretation of "hell" and "everlasting damnation." Because Jesus is not a "thief"! He wants to save and find those who are lost and give them life to the full.

Let's translate it in a better way: "and none of them was lost, except the son of *lostness*."

In connection to the passages mentioned, "lostness" opens yet another group of similar meanings. Our word, *apollymi,* is found also at the end of the encounter between Jesus and the chief tax collector, Zacchaeus (Lk 19:10): "For the Son of Man came to seek out and to save the lost [*apollōlos*]." Wonderful! The lost ones are the apple of God's eye! They are his favorites! He searches and saves them first – because God is all-encompassing, unconditional love.[21]

Was this not exactly what the sculptor in Vézelay chiseled in stone – for ages to come? Did perhaps the wise Peter the Venerable, if he was indeed the one who inspired the capitals, show these scripture passages to the sculptor to demonstrate that God is not a thief or a merchant or a day laborer – that God wants to give salvation?

---

21. This phrase of Jesus – it would be better for him (Judas) had he never been born – as I have explained, is in no way contradicting this. It can be interpreted "as through fire" or "purgatory" and therefore ultimately "salvation."

"For many" – "For all"?

Q7: Pope Benedict ordered the discontinuation of the phrase "for all," in the moment of transubstantiation, substituting it with "for many." That is how it is written in the Greek *urtext*, the primordial text of revelation. How can you speak of redemption also for Judas, possibly even for all? Could we say, then, that Maximilian Kolbe and Adolf Hitler will walk hand in hand in heaven?

A: Pope Benedict at the time referred to the Greek *urtext*, in which it is clearly stated: "this is my blood poured out for you and for *many*." The Lutheran New Testament scholar, Joachim Jeremias, interpreted this "many" as "all." Many Scripture scholars, both Lutheran and Catholic, followed him, and so the term "all" entered into our Mass texts. This word is incorrect.

Beyond the word itself, the question arises how this term "many" was understood and used in the Jewish environment of the time, beginning from the prophets before the exile, up to the time of Jesus. A correct translation can only be successful if one considers the *sense* of the word and the *linguistic usage* of the respective culture, in this case dating back centuries.

It might be that "many" and "all" shed light on each other (Norbert Lohfink). With the prophet Isaiah (2:2-3) we read exactly this: "*All* the nations shall stream to it. *Many* peoples shall come. . ."

"All" and "many" can therefore be set as parallels. The "all" is aimed for in "many," and the "many" opens up to "all," as happens over and over in Isaiah who speaks of "a covenant to the people, a light to the nations" (Is 42:6). In the second servant song he says again: "It is too light a thing that you should be my servant, to raise up the tribes of Jacob and restore the survivors of Israel; I will give you as a light to the nations, that my salvation may reach to the end of the earth" (Is 49:6).

The "many," therefore, grows into the "all." It opens up toward what is ahead.

The God and Father of our Lord Jesus Christ is not a tribal God. He did not want to bring salvation only to the small group of his people in the Mediterranean. He wanted, and will, through this small people, bestow salvation on the whole world, namely the many "peoples and kings." Therefore, the prophet Jeremiah is not only called to be a prophet for Jerusalem, but a prophet to "the nations" (Jer 1:5). Here we see the great theme of the pilgrimage of the nations to Jerusalem (Is 25:6): "The Lord of hosts will make for *all* peoples a feast of rich food, a feast of well-matured wines . . ."

These are a few examples of how God, through these prophets, opened the direction of the "many" to the "all." Jesus, the Son, who reposes at the heart of the Father, cannot fall short of his Father's revelations in the Old Testament. The "always greater love" is the measure for God's actions.

In the fourth servant song this becomes even more evident. As it is introduced, it speaks of "many nations" and "kings" (Is 52:15), who are startled and stand speechless, and at the end it says: ". . . yet he bore the sin of many, and made intercession for the transgressors" (53:12). The "many" is evolving here into a term with *dynamic* significance. The gaze is directed beyond all borders, beyond the horizon. These are the "many nations" of the book of Isaiah: with these "many," there will never be an end, neither concerning place, nor time, nor the offer of salvation.

Does not our faith contain the teaching of God's general will for salvation? God "desires everyone to be saved and to come to the knowledge of the truth" (1 Tm 2:4). To this end Jesus gave himself "a ransom for *all*" (1 Tm 2:6). Here the Semitic-dynamic "many" experiences its final form in the "all."

Furthermore, we need to take into consideration that the New Testament is not simply a linear continuation of the Old Testament, but a "new teaching – with authority" (Mk 1:27). It is a revelation of the fullness of the love of God. Jesus goes beyond the (only, or rather, static) "many." He gives to the last as much as to the first (Mt 20:14). Does it not then seem that Judas will be saved, too?

In the parable of the wedding feast it says: "'Therefore go into the highways, and as many as you find, invite to the wedding.' So those servants went out into the highways and gathered together all whom they found, both bad and good" (Mt 22:9-10 NKJV). A triple "all" is underlined by the literary positioning of the "bad" before the "good," as Jesus had already done in the Sermon on the Mount when he proposes a new "code of conduct," as opposed to what had been "told to your ancestors." In the sixth example, he concludes by saying that the Father in heaven "makes his sun rise on the evil and the good" (Mt 5:45), which means on *all*.

Luke takes this even further. Since there is still room in heaven (probably because only "many" are there), the owner sends the servant out one more time: "*Compel people to come in* so that my house may be filled" (Lk 14:23).[22]

The "gravitational power" of the infinite love of God will be irresistible. "When I am lifted up from the earth," Jesus says, "I will draw *all people* to myself" (Jn 12:32). At the same time, we will all be transformed (1 Cor 15:51)! Because of our freedom we will infinitely want God!

Why would we believe that God would reject even a single person, if he embraces the returning son, if he searches for the lost sheep, or the lost coin, until he finds them and carries them home to his feast? For the One who is eternal Love, there cannot be a cynical "Sorry, too late"! The "gravity" of his love brings about our transformation.

What Jesus had said ("The son of man came to seek out and to save the lost" [Lk 19:10]), Paul now brings into the beautiful phrase, that God imprisoned all in disobedience, that he may be merciful to all (Rm 11:32). The redemption of all people is the mystery of his will, which he has revealed to all the world (Eph 1:9-10). Of course, it is a great challenge for our natural human reasoning to imagine Maximilian Kolbe and Adolf Hitler as *transformed,* redeemed by this love, walking hand in hand! Maximilian Kolbe was transformed already

---

22. The following verse 24 seems to say the opposite: "None of those who were invited will taste my dinner (Greek: geusetai)." *Geuō* connotes to *savor, enjoy, like, approve of.* The verse could be interpreted as: "None of the men [Jesus speaks here to the leading Pharisees], who were called, will approve of/like my meal" or, none of them will "enjoy/savor my meal" – because I, Jesus, have called all those who did not deserve it, but on whom I want to bestow my gifts! Especially those who were called first obviously need a "heavenly rehab," before they, too, can savor the meal.

here on earth – but Hitler? As difficult as it may be, we cannot categorically deny to anyone the possibility of being transformed. Doesn't it say: "Love your enemies . . ." (Mt 5:44)? Could it be that even the worst person, the absolute worst, in the end is not excluded?

Naturally, we must not draw wrong conclusions from this for our earthly existence. To prevent people from committing crimes is a necessary aspect of Christian *love*. But the end goal is salvation for all – however and whenever it may be reached, after a serious and painful heavenly "rehab." Not to write off anyone definitely and permanently, is a change of perspective, an enormous challenge. When people begin to live with this new perspective, without being naïve, but decisively, many a vicious circle of violence can be broken.

This Good News, which exceeds our understanding because it is given to us from above, can and must be proclaimed, so that the face of the earth may be renewed according to the image of the One who formed it from his heart.

'The Good Shepherd of Vézelay'

Q8: Why can it be assumed that it is Jesus who is portrayed on the capital in Vézelay? Could it not be someone else?

A: Naturally, in images and often also in words, much is left to interpretation. In fact, one could say that the person on the left, depicted as hanged, is just an image of a person in despair, not Judas. There is no caption with a name written underneath. Many people have hanged themselves. This assumption would mean that, in the Church of St. Madeleine in Vézelay, some hanged person was depicted, and then, on the right side, some kind person is shown carrying the corpse somewhere . . . This hypothesis is possible but does not provide us with any reason for its existence.

If instead, it is the hanged apostle, Judas, depicted on the left, it would be inconsistent. It would make no sense, if, in the right half of the picture, just anyone were carrying the dead Judas somewhere.

Can we conclude then that it is Jesus? Jesus called himself the "Good Shepherd." This is established in Ezekiel where we hear of God as the shepherd of Israel (see Ez 34: 11-24). To my knowledge, no Jew before or after Jesus ever dared to call himself the "Good Shepherd," because by doing so, he would have made himself equal to the image of God in Ezekiel.

Because many other depictions show a shepherd carrying a sheep over his shoulders, we can assume that here it is Jesus who is carrying Judas.

In the sculpture, three things stand out about the person being carried. First: his face un-mistakenly shows a smile. Second: his hands are folded. One could be led to think that the "resurrection of Judas" is symbolized in that gesture! Third: the right (smiling) half of the face of the carried person fits exactly into the seemingly untouched right half of the face of the person carrying him . . . as though also Jesus were "redeemed," because he finally has his previously lost Judas with him. The merciful father surely laughed when he had his lost son home again, just as Jesus may have laughed in Zacchaeus' house, when he sat at the table with the lost one, to whom God had given salvation.

In this respect, the hypothesis that it may not be Jesus who carries the dead Judas home, seems thin to me. If nonetheless we assume that it is not Judas, what would be the result? Something wonderful!

Then, we would have *any person*, who carries *home any other person who has hanged himself*. One who is there for someone else in need. Did not Jesus in the parable of the Last Judgement (Mt 25:31-46) depict exactly this? "I was hungry . . ., I was homeless . . ., I was sick . . ., and you gave me . . ., you gave me . . ." The righteous people answered that it was not Jesus, but only this person or that one – in fact, *someone*! And the Creator and Redeemer of all mankind answers: "It was to *me* that you gave it!"

In this case, through this wonderful capital sculpture, the Lord would also tell us, too: "Give to your neighbor, no matter who he or she is, no matter what he or she did, give to your neighbor in need, what he or she needs now for their life. . .

". . .for eternal life with me."

Acknowledgements

This book would not have been published without the untiring thoroughness of my copy editor, Ms. Juliane von Magyary. She found the picture, enlarged it, produced the little images – and edited my text with theological intensity and spiritual breadth.

I want to thank my brother Johannes, who biked from Berlin to Vézelay and took the desired pictures. In the same way, I want to thank Monsieur Jean-Claude Gadreau for his photos. Thank you also to Neue Stadt Publishing House for transforming the photos.

A book is always the result of multiple collaborations and the product of long, contemplating inspections. Thus, it can become light for a thousand times more people. It is my wish that this may happen.